The Story of an Ordinary Father
Who Became an Unlikely Champion

TAKING ON DONAHUE AND TV MORALITY

Dr. Richard Neill

WITH LELA GILBERT

MULTNOMAH BOOKS

TAKING ON DONAHUE AND TV MORALITY

© 1994 by Richard Neill

published by Multnomah Books
a part of the Questar publishing family

Cover design by:
Donahue photo by: AP/Wide World Photos
International Standard Book Number: 0-88070-690-2

Printed in the United States of America

For information:
Questar Publishers, Inc.
Post Office Box 1720
Sisters, Oregon 97759

94 95 96 97 98 99 00 01 02 03 — 10 9 8 7 6 5 4 3 2 1

To Christi,
my precious wife of ten years,
who is my most ardent friend, encourager,
counselor, and companion, and
the mother of our three cherished gifts from God—
Lauri Ann, Natalie, and Greg.

Dear Reader,

We take our responsibility to you seriously. So we carefully considered whether we should include explicit material taken directly from Donahue's programs.

We decided we could not present the critical nature of this moral battle without presenting some of the degrading material that is daily broadcast into homes and minds by daytime TV. You may be shocked as we were. It is not our intent to sensationalize the material and certainly not to offend you, the reader, but to honestly inform you.

Our prayer is that you will respond, as we are, by taking a stand for our families, for our children.

Yours in the battle,

Don Jacobson
President and Publisher
Questar Publishers, Inc.

CONTENTS

ACKNOWLEDGMENTS

My special thanks to:

Christi, for your constant encouragement and help in monitoring Donahue broadcasts and for your spiritual and emotional support through very trying days.

Lauri Ann, Natalie, and Greg, who make coming home the highlight of my day. Because of you I was eager to remain on the front lines of the battle.

Lynda and Bob Beams, my tutors and cheerleaders from beginning to end.

El Arnold, a true warrior, who through his many contacts put me in touch with the right people at the right time.

Carol Bartley, an incredibly talented editor who had faith that my story was worth sharing.

All the people at Questar who by their efforts may enable others to make a difference in their communities.

Lela Gilbert, for creating a story from what read like a medical journal.

Dr. James Dobson, who gave me consistent inspiration and support.

The multitude of pro-family leaders across the country who stood with me and helped spread my vision.

CHAPTER ONE

How Did I Ever Get into This?

April 14, 1993. *I didn't want to get up out of bed today. Christi and I are waiting for the Phil Donahue Show to air this morning. Christi has monitored his show every day for the past year, but this time, there is a difference. This Donahue is not going to be about strippers, transsexuals, group sex parties, or sadomasochism. Today his show is about me—Dr. Richard Neill—and I'm more nervous than I want to admit.*

The *Phil Donahue Show* is normally broadcast from New York City. However, in recent days the production company had loaded up cameras, staff, and crew and headed south. The producers had rented the Tarrant County Convention Center in Fort Worth, Texas, where my family and I live. They had installed a bank of phones and made tickets available to three thousand Fort Worth residents. And to my chagrin, all this had happened because of me—a low-profile father of three, an introvert, and a nonconfrontational Christian layman.

Phil Donahue was about to confront me on national television because I didn't like what I saw on his shows.

For a solid year, I had been trying to get his broadcast moved from nine in the morning to a late night slot on the Dallas/Fort Worth ABC affiliate so children wouldn't be likely to watch his sexually explicit programming. I also had written thousands of letters, asking his advertisers to drop him because of the smut and sleaze on his shows.

Now, after months of silence, he finally had reacted, and reacted dramatically. By moving his entire operation to Fort Worth, he was attempting to stop my campaign because it was having a major financial impact on his program. From the sound of his recent radio and newspaper interviews, Donahue planned to put me on trial—my integrity, my ethics, my motives, my Christian beliefs—in front of more than ten million people. Needless to say, I had a knot in my stomach the size of a grapefruit.

I didn't sleep more than three hours the night before the broadcast. I kept telling myself, "Maybe Donahue will change his mind. Maybe at the last minute he'll decide he wants to feature something else on the program."

No such luck.

As the show started, about three thousand fans were in their seats, anxious to see Phil Donahue do his usual charismatic, magical performance. That day, his magic was intended to transform the reputation of Dr. Richard Neill from good guy to bad guy, and to make my campaign disappear.

When Donahue came out on stage, his first statement was, "We are pleased to be in Dallas/Fort Worth because this is the home of Dr. Richard Neill." A smattering of cheers could be heard from the crowd, but the overwhelming sound was loud, raucous boos. You could literally feel the crowd's anger. Someone was trying to remove Phil Donahue from their daily television diet, and they wanted no part of it.

How Did I Get into This?

When I was a kid, I occasionally watched wrestling, and those wrestling crowds made the strangest imaginable sounds. Donahue had put together a similar audience, but they were responding to a different kind of wrestling match: a great tug-of-war between good and evil. Even through the television set I could sense the spiritual warfare.

As I sat watching, I repeatedly asked myself, "How in the world did I ever get into this position?" At no point in my life had I imagined I would be the target of a personal attack, and certainly not a public one. I'm hardly a person who enjoys conflict. In fact, on the surface, I'm just the opposite—a quiet, reserved man whose idea of fun is going into the back room of my office and drilling holes in people's teeth. Now I was the one about to be drilled.

DONAHUE UPDATE: APRIL 27, 1992

Three women discuss their sexual escapades with an employer, a psychologist, and a pastor.

I have a wonderful wife, three great kids, a good job, a tremendous church, and everything else a person could ask for. Yet here I was, stirring up trouble, finding myself in the middle of a hurricane, at the mercy of a twenty-five-year television personality who was about to take me apart.

The broadcast began with Donahue playing a recording of an interview I had done with Dr. James Dobson of Focus on the Family. On the audiotape I was talking about my Christian beliefs and how those beliefs had, in part, motivated me to try to protect America's children from trash television. I was opening my heart to Dr. Dobson. But Donahue was trying to portray me as a cultlike figure—a Branch Davidian type on a holy mission. He wanted to depict me as a right wing religious zealot, not a concerned father or a good American citizen who cares about wholesome moral values.

Once the Dobson tape had played, Donahue went to the audience to launch a few more missiles my way. He asked them for their thoughts, and they went after me. I sat there thinking, "He isn't just upset. He's hot. He's getting poor write-ups in the local papers. He's seeing his sponsors drop like flies. He doesn't know what else to try, except to make an all-out verbal assault against me. And that's what he's doing."

It was really an ironic situation—I would have thought of myself as the least likely person on the planet to get into such a predicament. But as I sat there watching Donahue, I thought back on some other risky business I'd been involved in. In reality, "safety first" has never been my motto.

Marathon Man

When most people first meet me, they assume I'm a Type B personality—easy going, unruffled, and calm to the core. They come to this conclusion because I'm a slow talker and I don't anger easily. In actual fact, that's all rather deceiving. I'm actually a closet Type A. I get bored easily, love taking risks, and can easily become obsessive-compulsive. It wouldn't be difficult for me to become a workaholic.

It seems as if I've always searched for ways to get outside of my comfort zone, and sometimes that habit has not been in my best interest. This Donahue campaign, for example, certainly wasn't the most prudent project I've ever taken on. Yet God used the risk-taking part of me, that don't-get-too-comfortable aspect of my personality. In truth, I believe part of my personal drive has a deeply spiritual root—I know I'm not going to be on earth all that long, and I want to make the most of the time.

Sometimes, however, I get a little carried away.

Back in the early eighties, I started jogging because I wanted to get into better physical shape. The first day I jogged, I could hardly make it around the block. But the more I ran, the more I enjoyed it. I started running five-kilometer races and then ten. Next thing I knew, I was training for a marathon, although I'm still not sure why. I guess I wanted to see if I could do it.

I trained hard for about a year and half. And in 1987 I ran in a Fort Worth marathon and finished, which was a big victory for me. Then I injured my knee, and that was the end of my marathon career.

Near Miss on the Runway

All my life I had wanted to fly, and once I stopped running, I decided to take aviation lessons and to qualify for a private pilot's license. Since I didn't own a plane, I had to rent an aircraft. One day I rented a cheap Cessna 150, a real junker, and left Tyler, Texas, heading for Arlington. Just outside of Arlington, over some pastureland, the engine quit.

I was at approximately thirty-five hundred feet and immediately determined I'd better land the plane in the pasture. As I descended to seven hundred feet, the engine kicked back in, and the plane started upwards again. (Apparently the fuel line had clogged.) So I was able to get to the Arlington airport and get into the traffic pattern. Fortunately, no other planes were around.

Just as I was within sight of the runway, the engine quit again.

I didn't have enough altitude to make a proper approach, so I had to cut across the runway and land at a precarious angle. During the landing I didn't have time to think about how dangerous my flight had been. But once I got on the ground, I realized I had missed a barbed wire fence by about three feet and that at any point between Tyler and Arlington I could easily have been killed. It shook me up—but I didn't stop flying.

Swimming with the Sharks

In fact, fear has never stopped me from doing what I want to do. For example, before Christi and I were married, I was scuba diving off the coast of Monterey, California. The week before, there had been an article in the paper about a surfer being eaten by a shark. His body and surfboard had washed up on the beach, and huge, U-shaped bites were missing from both. Despite being a bit anxious, I couldn't resist diving anyway.

A kelp bed is like a big, underwater forest—you have no clear view of the waters around you. I'd never done this particular kind of diving before, so I was fascinated, although the thought of that hungry shark still lurked in my mind. As I descended, looking around eagerly, something suddenly nudged my fin. My heart literally stopped. As I jerked my head up to look behind me, I caught sight of a large sea creature.

A sea lion was playing with my flipper.

It occurred to me later on that day that dying from a heart attack was every bit as final as being eaten by a shark.

A Heart for Missions

My life really has been a paradox. I dread speaking in front of large groups. I have a fairly structured routine. I spend a lot of time with my family. I file my income taxes early. I do everything in a very calculated way. On the other hand, I persistently take on unlikely and seemingly uncharacteristic avocations.

Nonetheless, despite my penchant for adventure, I have never quite understood why God picked me to take on the *Phil Donahue Show*. It's one thing to risk danger when no one is looking. It's quite another to risk total humiliation on national television. The Lord certainly didn't choose me because of my debating skills. To make matters worse, I have a number of weaknesses. I tend to get cynical at times and see the worst in people. I can also be pessimistic. That's why God gave me a wife like Christi, who is an eternal optimist.

DONAHUE UPDATE: MAY 5, 1992

Several men describe sexual relations with
their mothers—incest in graphic detail.

In fact, it's interesting to look back and see where my life with Christi and my family was headed before the Phil Donahue campaign. In 1990 Christi and I felt God was calling us into some type of medical missionary work. I've always enjoyed missions and for a number of years have participated in a group that flies down to Mexico each year, providing dental work for the poor. That excursion never fails to exhilarate me, and because I enjoy it so much, I wondered if the Lord had something like that in mind for our family on a full-time basis.

I began to investigate opportunities in other countries and learned about a group of people who had formed a medical-dental clinic in the People's Republic of China. This clinic was founded as a joint venture between German investors and a Christian dentist in Singapore who is Chinese.

The chief of staff of the medical clinic, a missionary physician from the United States, was responsible for hiring. Through him, I learned the clinic was looking for a dentist. So in July 1991 Christi and I flew to Singapore to meet with the Christian dentist, and from there we went on to Beijing, China.

When we got off the airplane on the mainland, it was like taking a trip back into the 1930s. We shared a great sense of anticipation, because we knew we were right in the center of God's will. We toured the city and the clinic and explored housing and school opportunities. As Christi and I prayed extensively about being involved in the clinic, we both concluded it was, indeed, where God was leading us.

As soon as we returned to Texas, we began to make preparations for moving to Beijing in August 1992. We took language lessons in Mandarin. I put my practice on the market and soon found a potential buyer. We sent in the paperwork to enroll our daughters in the International School in Beijing. We located a suitable residence for us, our two girls, and our infant son, Greg. Everything was set—we were going to pack up, walk away from our good life in Fort Worth, and serve the Lord in Beijing, China.

An Unexpected Bend in the Road

Then, in March 1992, I received a fax from one of the clinic investors, informing me that the clinic was having financial problems because of corruption in the Chinese government and that the future didn't look good. Not many days later, we learned the clinic was closing.

I was discouraged and disappointed, yet I firmly believed God had good plans in store for Christi, the children, and me, and assumed it would be some other mission opportunity.

I couldn't have imagined what the future held—and how different it would be from my expectations. Within a matter of weeks I confronted my next assignment from the Lord. But it wasn't in China. Or Mexico. It didn't involve running, or scuba diving, or flying. But it required more of me than anything I'd ever done before, and involved issues and challenges I'd never even considered.

DONAHUE UPDATE: MAY 8, 1992

Seven men compare sexual exploits and numerous female partners.

God revealed to me an all new arena of ministry—moral campaigning and the fight against trash television—during a routine visit to a Fort Worth ophthalmologist in early April 1992.

That experience was the beginning of the campaign that brought Phil Donahue to Fort Worth. And it was my first step down a long, rough road that brought my concern for America's children to the attention of millions—including the ten million Donahue fans who were watching his show, along with me, that April morning almost exactly one year later.

CHAPTER TWO

My Mother Is a Slut

April 23, 1992. *Appointment with Dr. Marvelli for an eye exam. About twenty little children were sitting in his waiting room where Phil Donahue was on television, interviewing a "sex priestess."*

I n the early spring of 1992 I realized my eyes hadn't been examined for six or seven years. Since nobody wants a dentist who can't see well, I decided I better have my vision tested. A family emergency four or five years before had led us to Dr. Thomas Marvelli, an ophthalmologist in Fort Worth. He had willingly seen us on a Sunday after our oldest daughter, Lauri Ann, accidentally jabbed her finger in Christi's eye. Grateful for his professional concern and expertise, I had made a mental note to call on him again.

So I headed out for my eye appointment with my five-year-old, Natalie, along to keep me company. I look forward to taking one of our kids with me when I'm running errands because it's a great time to talk about things. Both girls beg to go with me, and I get a kick out of it.

As I signed in at the doctor's office, I noticed there were four people working behind the desk. From the perspective of being a doctor myself, my first thought was, "This is a very busy office." After I signed in, I was given a chart to fill out and directed to a waiting room.

The receptionist smiled, "We have two waiting rooms. You can have a seat in the one on the right, which is several doors down, or you can go to the one on the left-hand side."

This reaffirmed my earlier observation, "This is a very, very busy practice!" "How many doctors are there?" I asked. "Three or four?" "No, Doctor Marvelli is the only one, but he's very popular," she responded.

Natalie and I headed to the waiting room on the right side, turned the corner, and looked inside. Magazines covered the coffee tables—*Time, Newsweek, Better Homes and Gardens*. The atmosphere was relaxed. Several adults were reading quietly as elevator music played in the background. However, I needed to sit down to fill out the form and there weren't any empty chairs, so we turned to go.

The Children's Waiting Room

As we walked into the other waiting room, it didn't take long to figure out why all the adults were in the first one. This was the "padded cell" room—kids were everywhere. There had to be twenty children in that one room, with a lone adult who looked pretty frazzled. The only decor was the fingerprints on the walls and the shredded *People* magazines on the floor.

In one corner a little girl, who must have been about two, released an ear-piercing scream because another kid was pulling the head off of her doll.

A four-year-old was deeply engrossed with "Mr. Microphone." Now I'm an authority on Mr. Microphone. With this portable broadcasting system a child can sing or talk into the microphone and be heard all through the house. It's guaranteed to be turned up full blast at all times. The little boy was performing his own concert with Mr. Microphone, and he was making sure everybody in the building could hear him singing off-key at the top of his lungs.

On the couch sat several little girls holding a Kitty Surprise—a cat with the underside cut open, hollowed out, and stuffed with baby kittens about three inches long. As the child pulls the baby kittens out of the cat, it "gives birth" right there on the spot. Those little girls were giving birth to all those kittens, and at the time our girls wanted a Kitty

Surprise badly, so Natalie wasn't missing a thing.

I was trying to read a book to her in the midst of all the chaos—the boy's concert, the Kitty Surprise, and the toddler screaming because the doll was being decapitated. But it was so distracting we couldn't concentrate.

"My Mother Is a Slut"

Adding to the noise, a television was blaring on the other side of the room. Now I'm not a big television watcher because most of the programs seem like a mindless waste of time to me. But the volume was so high I couldn't block it out. Six small children were huddled around the screen, and one of the little guys must have been extremely nearsighted because his nose was all but touching the screen.

Unintentionally, I began to watch. I hadn't seen a *Phil Donahue* program for a number of years, although I had seen clips for *Donahue* and the other tabloid programs—sensational, sexually provocative excerpts intended to tease viewers into watching the daytime programming. Now, as I began to watch this program, my jaw literally dropped. The discussion centered around a woman who called herself the high priestess of sex, representing "The Church of the Most High Goddess," where sex is sacred. I could hardly believe my ears. She was saying, "I have sex for religious purposes—to purify people," and went on to report that she had participated in her "purification ritual" with 2,759 men. She even discussed in explicit detail having sex with more than one person at a time. The title of the broadcast, I later learned, was "My Mother Is a Slut."

DONAHUE UPDATE: JULY 7, 1992

Transsexuals talk about their sex-change operations. Donahue turns to the audience and asks, "I guess you want to know if it goes up and down."

While I was stunned, those little kids in Dr. Marvelli's waiting room were completely mesmerized. They were hanging on every word.

I jumped up and changed channels, and the kids quickly adjusted to the cartoon that appeared on the screen, their attention thoroughly diverted. I hoped they could forget what they'd seen. But I couldn't. At that very moment I was catapulted from my complacency, from my comfort zone. Right then and there I realized, "Enough is enough. I've got to do something." Only one thing was lacking—I didn't have a clue what that would be.

Like many people in America, I really didn't think anything could be done about the things that offended me. Many of us are concerned. We love God; we love our families; we love our country. We are concerned about the decline in values and about the moral free fall that is evident wherever we look. Many of us would gladly act if we thought we could have any impact at all. I was just one concerned parent. I was just one busy businessman. I was just one deeply offended consumer. But I soon discovered I could make my voice heard, and I'm writing this book to let you know you can make your voice heard, too.

Although I didn't know it yet, God was going to use my brief time in that waiting room full of children and that shocking *Donahue* broadcast to totally change my life. As I left Dr. Marvelli's office that day, I thought, "I have perfect vision, but if I watched much more of this stuff on television, I would have to have my brain examined. That kind of sleaze could warp your mind."

The Reluctant Churchgoer

Saturday, April 25, 1992. *A beautiful sunny day—not a cloud in the sky. Didn't plan to, but went to church tonight. Met Lynda Beams, who was successful in getting Geraldo Rivera off the air in Dallas— single-handedly.*

The last thing I expected to do that Saturday was go to church. We had been working in the yard all day, and not because I have a green thumb, either. I lose five or six shrubs every winter, and this was my Saturday to purchase new ones and replace the ones that had died. Late in the afternoon Christi said, "Tonight at church some speakers are coming to talk about getting active in moral issues. I think it's going to center around what can be done to improve television."

To be perfectly honest, I really wasn't interested in going. My no-longer-white tennis shoes were ripped and green with grass stains, and my jeans were tattered around the edges. I was in no shape to go anywhere, especially not to church. "The meeting is going to be at 6:45," Christi said.

I immediately reacted. "There's no way! It's 6:30 now. It takes us twenty minutes to get to the church, so we'd be late. Besides, we don't have time to clean up." I thought that would be the end of it.

About ten minutes later Christi said, "I really would like to go to that meeting at church, especially after what you told me about that *Donahue* program the other day. You might enjoy listening to this."

DONAHUE UPDATE: JULY 9, 1992

A guest discusses having sex with several partners simultaneously.

I was worn out from all the yard work, but I said, "I'll go if you'll agree to get there late and leave early. That way we won't have to talk to anybody. We'll sit at the back, and we'll get in and out quickly without being seen." Needless to say, I was self-conscious about my appearance—nobody wants a bum for a dentist.

When we arrived at the church, a crowd of about two hundred people was present. It was obvious that everyone was listening intently. For one thing, they were all down at the front, which in a Southern Baptist Church is really unusual. Most of the time the front five or six pews are empty. But on that particular evening, the first twenty rows were packed. As I began to watch and listen, I realized these people weren't coming just to be entertained but were deeply concerned parents who wanted to make a difference in society. The speakers talked about current issues in Texas—issues that were impacting families in a negative way—and also some opportunities that would impact the family in a positive way.

Until that night, I had somehow managed to tune out such discussions.

A Woman Named Lynda Beams

The person who most captured my attention was a lady named Lynda Beams. Single-handedly she had taken Geraldo Rivera off the air in Dallas/Fort Worth. When I heard that, my ears perked up. It had happened three years earlier, and I had never heard a word about it. That shows you where I was on moral issues. It had happened in my own backyard, and I didn't even know it.

As planned, Christi and I left early. But after we went to bed that night, I lay awake for two hours, wondering if the same thing could be done with the *Donahue* program. The more I thought about it, the more I realized that, no, it would never work. My final thoughts as I drifted off to sleep were, "No. That's nonsense. Not Donahue. He's got the top-rated program in the Dallas/Fort Worth area. He's the king of talk show television."

In retrospect, I can see great irony in that first sleepless night. Until then, once I hit the sack, I was gone—out like a light—and always slept eight to nine hours a night. Even if I'd been told, I would never have believed how dramatically my sleep patterns were soon to be disrupted. Before long I would be staying up late at night, working on this document, thinking through that strategy, and staring at thousands of letters through red-rimmed eyes.

The next morning Lynda Beams was in the church service again, sitting close to the front. After church, Christi and I went up and introduced ourselves. I was expecting to encounter someone like Bella Abzug, Eleanor Smeal, or Molly Yard of the Amazon Battalion—loud and aggressive—but when Christi and I were face to face with Lynda, we found her to be a humble and gracious person. She was not a braggart but simply a godly individual who was determined to do what she could to positively impact society.

We explained that we were quite interested in what she had accomplished and that we very much admired her efforts in taking on

Geraldo. Then I took a deep breath and said, "Do you think the same thing could be done with Donahue?"

Her eyes lit up, and she smiled. "There's no doubt in my mind it could work over and over and over again! It's a repeatable process, a cookbook approach. I know you could do it!"

After we talked for five or ten minutes, I felt as if we were taking too much of her time. "I know you need to get home to your family, but could we give you a call some time next week?" I asked.

"Sure," she nodded and gave us her telephone number. Then we left.

We had lunch, and Christi and the kids went to take Sunday afternoon naps, but I couldn't get the thought out of my head: could this be done with another program? Instead of waiting until later in the week, I called Lynda right then. I was amazed by her willingness to talk to me at length—we talked for about four hours that day—and to help me lay out a plan of action for taking on the *Donahue* program.

Lynda is a consistently positive person, particularly when it comes to campaigns like hers and mine. She didn't say, "I'm not sure, but it might work again." She didn't say, "If this works,"or, "We'll just have to wait and see if this works." She said, "It *will* work. I know it!" Then she went on to develop a strategy with me, based on all she had learned during her experience with Geraldo.

The Making of an Activist

For me, this was an extraordinary situation. I had never been an activist in any kind of a campaign. It was completely out of character for me to pursue this. I know it was God's prompting because I had absolutely no desire to take on such a confrontational, controversial mission.

For one thing, our family's course had been set in an altogether different direction. We were involved in missions—not only the China clinic, but other evangelistic and discipleship activities, like prison work and local Bible studies. Moral issues, like abortion and pornography and Christians in politics, had been important to me, but I'd never given them my attention. I figured, "There's only so much time in the day, and my efforts wouldn't make a difference anyway."

For me, that's proof positive that God laid the Donahue challenge on my heart.

Monday, April 27, 1992. *Talked to Brother Miles. Not sure whether he thinks I'm doing the right thing or not.*

I personally think I've got the best pastor in the world. I've been inspired and encouraged by Miles Seaborn's preaching for ten years. He has always preached the word of God, but he has also encouraged people to get active in the community, to try to improve society, to spread Truth, and to disciple the people who accept Christ. He has such a heart for the Lord. Before coming to our church, he was a missionary in the Philippines for ten years.

As a result, a number of people in our church are quite active in moral concerns: fighting pornography, abortion, and outcome-based education. Miles has always encouraged his congregation to keep an eternal perspective about life, which is the only way to make moral campaigns work because they involve an enormous amount of hard work and spiritual confrontation. They certainly aren't worth the trouble if our eyes are fixed solely on enjoying our earthly existence to the maximum.

Because of the positive contributions he's made in my life, I wanted to talk to Miles about my ideas regarding Phil Donahue. I valued his counsel and knew I needed his prayers. Of course I could well imagine what I'd do in his shoes if somebody told me he was going to take on Phil Donahue. I would probably say, "That's real nice and I am really proud of you," all the while thinking, "Yeah, right! This will never, never work."

When I reached Miles by phone, I explained to him what I had been thinking. I said, "I feel God has laid it on my heart to take on the sleaze programming on the *Phil Donahue Show*, so that's what I've decided to do. Christi and I have prayed about it."

DONAHUE UPDATE: JULY 12, 1992

A lesbian describes oral sex using a dental dam.

A long silence on the other end of the phone. "Well, that sounds good," he finally said, but his voice wasn't convincing. I wasn't at all sure he thought I was doing the right thing. At the end of the conversation, he remarked, "Well, to be forewarned is to be forearmed. I'll be praying for you, and as a church we will support you in every way we can." Again I could sense his hesitancy, and as I hung up the phone, I thought, "He must know something I don't." In fact, he was all too aware of the difficulties ahead. I had a lot to learn about spiritual warfare.

"Fruitless Deeds of Darkness"

Next I called my friend David Miller, the Tarrant County director for the American Family Association. Here was somebody else I respected for being on the cutting edge of moral issues, and I wanted to bounce some ideas off him. Although he was very encouraging over the phone, I could tell he thought I was a bit crazy to be taking on Phil Donahue. As I talked to several people that day, I felt that a lot of them were humoring me. But I was energized, regardless of what anybody thought.

When I went to the office Monday, my enthusiasm was so high I had a hard time working. Usually I'm so intent on what I'm doing that I don't think about anything else all day. In fact, I take a lot of pride in doing the best job I can possibly do technically. But that Monday I was having a hard time concentrating. Fortunately we didn't have any tedious procedures to deal with—mostly exams and consultations and people with toothaches.

I had decided to monitor *Donahue,* so I was eager to get home to find out what had aired that morning. I remember thinking, "I'm sure it was a wholesome program today." Wrong! There on the tape was

Donahue interviewing three women who discussed having sex with a boss (on the window sill), a psychotherapist (on a towel), and a minister (on the floor of his office). The details were graphic and appalling. The more I watched, the more I increased my resolve to accomplish this task God had given me. That night I went to bed with a passage of scripture playing and replaying in my head, a passage Christi had mentioned to me when we first began talking about the *Donahue* broadcast the Thursday before. With every passing hour it took on more meaning. Two thousand years ago Paul wrote these words to the early Christians. Could anything be more relevant today?

> Have nothing to do with the fruitless deeds of darkness, but rather expose them. For it is shameful even to mention what the disobedient do in secret. But everything exposed by the light becomes visible, for it is light that makes everything visible. This is why it is said: "Wake up, O sleeper, rise from the dead, and Christ will shine on you." Be very careful, then, how you live—not as unwise but as wise, making the most of every opportunity, because the days are evil (Ephesians 5:11-16).

CHAPTER THREE

When Is Enough, Enough?

Tuesday, April 28. *Talked at length with Lynda Beams. She explained specific principles for launching a campaign. This is going to be a major commitment!*

After another day at work, examining teeth, consulting with patients, and trying desperately to keep my mind on dentistry, I again called Lynda Beams and her husband, Bob. Our previous conversations had mostly addressed generalities, presented with Lynda's and Bob's optimism, but now I was ready to take another step forward. I wanted to find out exactly what would have to be done—the-nuts-and-bolts details—if I were to launch a campaign.

Although we will look at them in more detail later, it's important to get an overview of the guidelines, the essential building blocks, for any successful campaign.

PRINCIPLE #1:
GET ORGANIZED

Fortunately, I'm an organizer by nature; that's one of my strong points. And if you aren't, it's critical you become one—that you force yourself to develop a system—at the very beginning. A campaign to take on a television show cannot be completed quickly; it's a commitment for at least a year. So you have to be organized in everything you do—the development of charts as well as the discipline of your daily life, which allows time to get the job done. It won't seem important at first, but a year down the road it will be a lifesaver.

My first few lists weren't well thought out; they weren't computerized or alphabetized. Before long, I realized they were inadequate, so Christi and I changed our course.

Our first chart was of the dates certain topics were discussed on *Donahue* broadcasts and any obscenity involved. All the broadcasts were listed sheet by sheet. This is important documentation because sometimes an advertiser will call to deny that the program cited contained obscenities or that their commercials appeared on that program. In order for your argument to be convincing, accurate records of the programs' content and advertisers must be available at a moment's notice. Also, in doing media interviews, it's important to be able to update the media on any recent examples of obscenity on the program.

Topics Discussed on Donahue

Date	Subject of program	Obscenity
10-22	Call girls	
10-25	Hollywood hookers	
10-27	Could you kill for your kids?	

Our second chart was an alphabetized list of each product or company that advertised on the *Donahue* program each day. However, the sponsoring company for the product may not be obvious. For example, a product such as Crest toothpaste or Listerine will be advertised, and you'll have to research where the product is made and by whom. You can do that by going to the grocery store and checking the printed information on the packaging. We also listed on this chart the length of the commercial—fifteen, thirty, or sixty seconds—to show the advertiser's financial commitment. And we noted whether the advertisement was local or national in scope. You can usually determine by the quality of the ad whether it's sponsored by a local food store, car dealership, or convenience store, or whether it's a national ad for a major corporation like Revlon or Montgomery Ward.

Sponsors

Product Advertised	Date	Length	Local/National
Accutrim III	1-14		
Airwick Stick Ups	5-5		
Alka Seltzer	11-9		
	12-2		

Our third chart listed manufacturers and the products each company makes. Some of these companies make one product, others make dozens. If you aren't able to access this information on your own, the American Family Association in Tupelo, Mississippi, will provide you with resource materials that can be extremely helpful. Ask for *The Fight Back Book.*

Companies and Products

Company	Product Made
Abbott Labs, parent company of Ross Labs	Murine Eye Drops
Alberto-Culver USA, Inc. Melrose Park, IL 60160	FDS
American Cyanamid (Lederle labs)	Centrum Vitamins

PRINCIPLE #2:
DEVELOP A LONG-TERM VISION

I remember innocently asking Lynda, "How long did it take you to get Geraldo off the air in the Dallas/Fort Worth area?" assuming she would say, "Oh, three or four months." When she said, "Eighteen months," reality began to dawn. This campaign was going to be my life for the next couple of years or more.

It's vital to have a long-term vision of any campaign, whether it is on moral issues or political ones. That's diametrically opposed to most things in our fast-paced, have-it-in-an-instant culture. If we don't want to cook, we can drive to a fast-food restaurant and pick up something to eat. We can flip on a television or a computer and find just about anything we want to know, right at our fingertips. As people raised in a high tech world, our attention span seems to be appallingly short.

In fact, our long-term vision needs to extend all the way to an eternal perspective. We're not working simply to accomplish goals for this present world, even though some of the improvements would help future generations here on earth. We're working for our heavenly Father and our Savior.

Again, I remember asking Lynda in my naiveté, "How many sponsors had to pull out of the *Geraldo* show before they took him off the air in the Dallas/Fort Worth area?" (I thought she'd say fifteen or twenty.) "A hundred and seven," came the reply.

My first thought was, "God is going to have to do this. There's no way, humanly speaking, I can get over a hundred sponsors—huge, invincible, corporate advertisers—to withdraw from the *Donahue* program. His ratings are sky-high. That can't be done without God's intervention." In that particular conclusion, I was absolutely right!

Tackling this kind of campaign is like being a marathon runner. A marathoner trains for months, sometimes years, and is highly disciplined. When he gets up in the morning, he knows exactly what he has to accomplish in the next sixteen hours. While he is training, he envisions himself running the race, finishing it in a prescribed time, and probably even crossing the finish line in first place. He is focused on one competition; he doesn't train for ten other events simultaneously. In the same way, you can't take on ten disgusting television shows at once. Emotionally, spiritually, and logistically, you couldn't handle it. Like a runner, you simply have to take things a step at a time and stay focused on the finish line.

PRINCIPLE #3:
PRAYER COMES FIRST

I can't encourage you strongly enough to begin your campaign with prayer. It's so necessary to seek God's counsel and protection and to receive His guidance. This became a spiritual struggle for me, even though I've had a quiet time every morning for years. It isn't always a "mountaintop experience;" sometimes it's dry and other times it's rich. But I'm committed to my daily time with God, and I never would have spiritually survived the campaign without it. As Lynda told me early on, "Unless you realize this is going to be the Lord's doing, you are going to lose right off the bat. The spiritual warfare is too intense." How true!

PRINCIPLE #4:
DEVELOP A PETITION

The formulation of a petition serves more than one purpose. A petition not only makes the community aware of our efforts, but it makes the issue a community concern. One purpose of my petition drive was to say, "This is not just Richard Neill out here trying to get *Donahue* changed, and Richard Neill isn't simply a loose cannon. He has a lot of support. He's got lots of good company."

It isn't difficult to get thousands of names on petitions, and those names will accomplish a great deal. In the beginning, a petition drive brings public awareness to your campaign. Then, later on, the names you've collected will become valuable contacts. You'll be able to use the addresses to let people know how things are going and to enlist their continued support. Lynda was able to get eleven thousand signatures on petitions regarding Geraldo by spending months and months going to doctor's offices, churches, stores—anywhere else she could think of. Since I have a dental practice to run, I had to devise a way to get the petitions in the hands of people without having to do all the legwork myself. More on that later.

DONAHUE UPDATE: JULY 13, 1992

A look at strippers in their seventies and eighties.

PRINCIPLE #5:
CREATE A VIDEOTAPE

Lynda explained to me the importance of making a videotape which would visually present the most telling *Donahue* excerpts. Many corporate advertisers don't know what they are sponsoring, and this tape helps convince them the shows are truly objectionable and that it will be bad for business if they continue to channel their advertising dollars into provocative and offensive programming.

When Lynda made her Geraldo tape, she simply put two VCRs together and recorded clips from one VCR to another. According to her, the video was so homemade looking it was almost funny. But that's not necessarily bad. Advertisers and the media will realize quickly this is a one-person campaign when they see the video. My original video was only twenty-one minutes long and was technically rough. However, it worked, and worked well.

Don't worry about the quality of your tape, as long as it's viewable and the key clips are there. I had clips from five different programs that had aired over a two-week period. At the opening of the video I placed a title that said, "Please Watch through the Eyes of a Child." I wanted the sponsors to imagine a child, perhaps their own child, watching some of Donahue's programs about strippers, transsexuals, sado-masochism, homosexual weddings, and men having sex with their mothers. It took about three days to put the video together and it was obviously homemade, but it was extremely powerful. I sent the finished product to some of the sponsors; to others I just mentioned in my original letter that a video was available.

PRINCIPLE #6:
CONTACT THE LOCAL BROADCASTER

Lynda explained that I should send a letter to the local television station manager. In my case, that meant writing to the president of the local ABC affiliate, WFAA. When I wrote, I appealed to him to move the broadcast to a late night time slot. Lynda warned me, "This is a formality. Of course they're not going to move the show, and you might as well count on it. But you need to send that letter so down the road you can show you gave them a warning." In other words, don't write the advertisers before you've given the station a chance to pull out.

PRINCIPLE #7:
MONITOR THE BROADCASTS

My next step was to monitor the *Donahue* program *every day*. It's critical that this be done daily and that the charts be filled out because you may have to show evidence, at a moment's notice, of what advertisements appeared on a program. This also provides eyewitness evidence of the crude and shocking material being exploited on the shows.

PRINCIPLE #8:
RALLY SUPPORT

When General Schwarzkopf went into the Gulf War, he didn't head for Iraq by himself. He didn't dash out into the desert sand, brandishing a pistol in each hand, and single-handedly take on Saddam Hussein's troops. He rallied his troops and put together his biggest guns, ships, planes, and missiles. When he finally confronted the enemies, he blew them away.

A campaign against a television program is also a war on foreign soil, and it is equally important to rally your support and mobilize the troops. In the beginning, I called a number of pro-family organizations, like Concerned Women for America, the Dallas Association For Decency, Eagle Forum, the American Family Association, Focus on the Family, and Christian Coalition. I also called the PTA and a number of other civic and church organizations. At the outset, I contacted these organizations to enlist their support in name only; I didn't ask them actually to *do* anything. I simply asked, "May I mention your name in my letter to the sponsors and say you agree with what I'm doing?"

Several organizations wanted to see what I was sending to the advertisers, and once they found out, they were eager for me to use their names. They couldn't have agreed more heartily that the material is not suitable for young children (or, for that matter, for adults!). Before the campaign was over, a number of these organizations wrote newsletter articles which named several *Donahue* sponsors. As I worked at rallying support, I discovered a core group of people who stand strong for traditional family values and the Judeo-Christian ethic. Unfortunately this core of men and women contains only a minority of the churchgoers. Many believers simply aren't interested in fighting cultural evils.

PRINCIPLE #9:
MAKE USE OF THE MEDIA

The last thing on earth I ever wanted to deal with was the media—Christian or secular. However, Lynda explained that both secular and Christian media are essential to the campaign since the media is an avenue for getting the message out to millions of people across the country. In fact, not only should you talk to the media, you should talk through them.

Generally the Christian media is going to ask you the right questions and help you give the right answers. You can share both your heart and your spiritual concerns with most Christian interviewers. On the other hand, some journalists in the secular media may be out to get you, so you must have your message down pat before you make it public. Determine exactly what you want people in a lost world to hear about what you're doing. If you position yourself carefully, the secular media will be less likely to give a distorted view of you and your goals in the campaign. As you develop your strategy (see Principle #12), you'll be considering this subject of positioning.

During our long and complex conversation, nothing Lynda said concerned or intimidated me more than this. I remember remarking, "I don't think I can deal with it. I wonder if this campaign can be carried out without any media attention."

"I really don't think so," she responded. Once again, she was absolutely right.

DONAHUE UPDATE: JULY 16, 1992

Program subject: "Sex—Three Times a Day"

PRINCIPLE #10:
CONTACT CORPORATE ADVERTISERS

One point here needs to be especially clear—corporations are our friends in a campaign like this. They hold the keys to keeping Donahue—or anybody else—on the air or taking him off. They have the power. Furthermore, many of the advertising executives are family men and are not the media elite of New York City or Hollywood. They are simply businessmen, trying to make a profit for their company, and they have a job to do.

I am convinced, after reading a number of the responses I received from these advertisers, that they, too, want to make America a better country. Many expressed a genuine desire to help out once they were convinced a program was offensive and morally inappropriate.

PRINCIPLE #11:
USE THE "PUBLIC FILE" AND THE FCC

Each television and radio station is required by the Federal Communications Commission (FCC) to keep a "public file," a file of all letters of protest or support of a particular program that the station has received. As the campaign progresses, encourage people to write to the station manager of the local station you are challenging. Their letters of protest will go into the public file and will be taken into consideration by the FCC when the station's license is up for renewal. There will also be an appropriate time in the campaign to get supporters to file complaints with the FCC This is an excellent way to put pressure on the local station because it does not want pressure from the FCC.

PRINCIPLE #12:

STICK TO YOUR STRATEGY

Strategy is a big word in a public campaign, for several reasons. For one thing, it gives you a clear and concise set of issues to address. For another, strategy keeps you from waffling around and going off on tangents. It helps you answer difficult questions within a narrow framework and keeps you from getting mired down in peripheral issues.

My first step in developing a strategy was to concern myself specifically with the well-being of latchkey children, who have no parental supervision. You might consider a similar approach for your campaign, for the following reasons. If you go into a campaign saying, "This is terrible subject matter; no one should be watching it," critics will question, "Who are you to impose your morals on other people? Everybody has the right to watch what he or she wants." If you focus the campaign only on children, saying, "I want it moved to late night because it's not fit viewing for children," then critics will say, "Don't you think it's the parents' responsibility to monitor what their children can watch?" However, if you focus on latchkey children—children who are left unattended while their parents are at work, who come home from school and flip on a television while both parents are absent—that argument is invalid.

My second strategy was *not* to insist the *Donahue* show be taken off the air altogether. Instead I simply asked that it be moved to a late night time slot. Some of my critics actually came to my defense and said, "Look, he's just trying to get the time of the show changed. Give him a break. He's not trying to get it off the air." I knew full well that the local affiliate would probably not change the time of the program. They were more likely to cancel it than move it. The audience for *Donahue* is primarily housewives and elderly people, and if the time were changed to late night, the station would lose its audience. However, if by chance they did move the show to late night, I would have to stick to my word and stop the campaign.

Another strategy decision I made was to handle the campaign on my own rather than as part of a group. In the beginning I had approached several organizations about waging a campaign against *Donahue*, offering to do the work myself if they would be out front. But I was advised against pursuing that course. Allen Wildmon, who is with the American Family Association and is a veteran of many television campaigns, advised, "Richard, if you really want to be successful with this campaign, you need to go into it all alone."

I didn't like that. I didn't want to hear that. I wanted a lot of other people facing the confrontations with me. But Wildmon's reasoning made a lot of sense. He said, "If you go into it with a big group, the media is going to have a huge target to throw rocks at, and they'll do it. But if you go into it alone and position yourself as a concerned father, the media will understand that and will give you a break. They love David and Goliath stories. You're a nobody, and it's going to be hard for them to throw rocks at you when you don't have a name."

It has served me well to position myself as the little guy. I've tried to do my work quietly, not seeking a lot of publicity and keeping myself as anonymous as possible.

I've been asked several times, "Do you think having 'Dr.' in front of your name was an advantage in this campaign?" And my answer is no. Lynda Beams was a housewife. She didn't type. She didn't have a computer. And she got Geraldo completely off the air in the Dallas/Fort Worth area. I don't think "Dr." is necessary at all.

Seeking God's Help and Guidance

Wednesday, April 29. *After talking to Lynda yesterday, the full scope of this campaign is beginning to sink in. Am I really going to do this?*

The first thing I realized when I woke up that spring morning was the enormity of the campaign I was taking on.

Since having a personal spiritual revival in 1988, I have made it a point to get up every morning and have a quiet, devotional time in our den. For up to an hour, I study the Bible, pray, and seek God's guidance. That morning I said, "Lord, I need your direction. And there's no question—you will get 100 percent of the glory from this campaign. You are the only One who knows the size of this task and what's going to be involved. You are the only One who can see the future. You're the only One who knows what kind of trouble I'm going to get into with the media. You are the only One who knows if I'm going to be sued or if there will be physical threats to me or my family. I'm just going to place this totally in Your hands."

I asked God to soften the hearts of the sponsors and the executives at WFAA. I asked Him to touch the heart of Phil Donahue himself, and I prayed for his salvation. With Phil Donahue's power, what great things he could do for the Lord.

Broadcast Information—in Black and White

During lunch that day, I called Journal Graphics in Denver, Colorado, the producers of the transcripts for the *Donahue Show*. (Their phone number is broadcast at the end of the show.) Rather than monitor the show for the next several months, I decided this was a more practical way to get started quickly and to bring me up to speed on what had happened in recent months.

I said, "This is Richard Neill, and I would like to order the last six months of *Donahue* transcripts."

"The past six months? That's almost 120 transcripts!" the man responded.

"That's okay. How much are they?"

"Well, normally they're five dollars, but since you are ordering so many, we'll give them to you for three dollars apiece."

"Great!"

"Incidentally, maybe it's none of my business, but why do you want this many transcripts?"

I explained, "Well, I'm monitoring the content of *Phil Donahue*, and I want to make a report."

"Oh, okay," he replied without further concern. Apparently no one had taken on Donahue before, so he didn't seem suspicious.

That same day Christi began to monitor *Donahue* daily.

A Good Reason to Care

That night I called El Arnold, the president of the Dallas Association for Decency, a man who was to become a mentor to me. One of the first things he said was, "Tell me about your family. How many children do you have?"

"Three," I responded.

He asked how old they were, and then he said, "That's your reason for doing this, isn't it?"

I said, "Yeah, that's right. That is why I'm doing this. For my kids and for other kids, too—our future generations."

That came home to me the next day as I was watching our son, Greg, while Christi ran errands. At six months old, Greg wasn't crawling yet; I could lay him on the floor, and he would watch me as I worked at the computer. The girls were out riding their bikes in front of the house, enjoying a beautiful spring day, and I was sitting in my study in the house, writing letters, making phone calls, and following up on details. For the first time, (but certainly not the last!) I thought, "What in the world are you doing this for? Why are you sitting in here when you could be outside spending time with your kids?"

I glanced down, and there lay Greg, smiling up at me. I said aloud,

"That's right. That's exactly why I'm doing this! I'm doing this for him." I looked out the window again, and as I watched the girls riding around outside, I realized, "I'm doing this to try to make a better world for them. There will be days when I will have more time to spend with them, but today God wants me to do this."

DONAHUE UPDATE: AUGUST 3, 1992

Several women report being raped by their husbands.

More Shocking Donahue Shows

In the next few days *Donahue's* broadcasts fell like heavy blows upon my consciousness. Even now I haven't become accustomed to the sexually explicit material he showcases. I hope I never do.

On *Donahue's* May 5, 1992, show several men discussed in graphic detail their experiences in having sex with their mothers.

On May 8, 1992, *Donahue* featured seven men who bragged about how many women they have had sex with. One man had been a centerfold in a women's pornography magazine. Another was a male stripper, who estimated he had slept with over two thousand women.

That same day I received the *Donahue* transcripts I had ordered from Journal Graphics, and I began the laborious job of reading them. As I studied the thick pile of papers, a heavy oppression began to weigh on me. Once Phil Donahue's charisma and humor were removed, the cold, ugly facts about his broadcasts stared back at me in black and white.

I stayed up until half past three that morning, reading transcripts and developing my report, determined to get through them as quickly as possible. I read about sadomasochism, adults having sex with minors, transsexuals discussing their sex change operations, strippers, and people who arranged group sex parties. I realized, sadly, that millions of housewives are hooked on this stuff.

Reading and reporting such filth was not a pleasant task, but I told myself again and again that long night: "If you're going to make a report for your campaign, you've got to be explicit. You can't water it down." I used actual quotes and cited specific details, the most graphic details I could find in the transcripts. I also made sure they were used in the context of the program. By the time I finished, I had written a three-page report—an appalling, sickening compilation of material I could hardly bear to think about. The truth about Phil Donahue's broadcasts was worse than I had imagined.

As I stacked up my papers and switched off the computer, I thought about each of my children, sleeping peacefully in their rooms, and imagined how I'd feel if they were exposed—even once—to the kinds of things I had just read and reported. My stomach tightened, and the very thought sickened me.

"Enough is enough," I resolved as I headed for bed, weary and disgusted. "Just one little kid seeing that garbage is one kid too many."

CHAPTER FOUR

Going Public with the Campaign

Thursday, April 30, 1992. *Wrote to David Lane at WFAA and formulated a petition. These two major steps should open many new doors for the campaign.*

As I mentioned in the last chapter, before contacting any advertisers, it was expedient for me to write to the general manager of WFAA, the Dallas ABC affiliate, to give the station fair warning that I was concerned about the *Donahue* programming. It would provide them with an opportunity to respond, before I took further steps.

Mr. Lane responded two weeks later. He stated that since very few children watched *Donahue* in the Dallas/Fort Worth market, he didn't feel a time change was warranted. Most station managers are accustomed to getting letters like mine, and they have a form letter prepared in response. They know that people are usually angry about something, and once they vent it, most drop the subject. In fact, few people write a second letter. They say, "I've done my duty. I've written to the station, and that's all I can do."

Fortunately, when I received Mr. Lane's letter, I felt no emotional letdown. Lynda Beams had prepared me for his response, and I was now free to contact the *Donahue* advertisers, once I had done my petition work. That same day I worded and reworded the petition until I had it the way I wanted it.

May 10, 1992

David Lane, President
WFAA-TV
Communications Center
606 Young Street
Dallas, TX 75202

Dear Mr. Lane:

I am writing you to express my frustration and to
appeal to you for help.

I am becoming increasingly alarmed by the sexually
explicit nature of the Donahue Show. His programs
recently featured sadomasochism, strippers, a
homosexual wedding, and discussions about group
sex parties. I am sure you will agree that this
is adult programming.

Undoubtedly you will agree that our future generations are our most valued resource and that the
issue of children's access to inappropriate television programming is a very serious matter.
Children's minds are like sponges. Anything they
soak in will affect their thoughts for the rest
of their lives.

For these reasons, I am requesting that WFAA
change the time of the Donahue Show to a late
night hour, between eleven in the evening and five
in the morning, to minimize the viewing by children. As you know, it presently airs during daytime hours.

I am asking that you respond to this request
within ten days.

Sincerely,

Richard B. Neill

Friends Who Care and Pray

On May 10, Bob and Lynda Beams invited Christi and me, and El and Jeanne Arnold, to lunch. We had all met by phone, but this was our first face-to-face encounter with the Arnolds. At the meeting it was clear that these Christians had their minds on eternal things. They were genuinely concerned about making our world a better place for our children and for generations yet to be born.

The six of us began to strategize, and before we parted, we had developed several goals. One was to have four *Donahue* sponsors withdraw by October 1. Could any of us have guessed that seventy-one sponsors would withdraw by that date? At the end of the meeting, we prayed together around the table, asking the Lord to bless the campaign.

That luncheon meant more to me than I could express. Here were people I hardly knew taking the time to help me, to give me sound advice, and to support me spiritually. The fact that they were people I sincerely admired made their contributions even more significant.

Plans to Meet the Media

Another goal we set that day was to keep the campaign quiet with the secular media as long as possible. Perhaps at some later date we would contact the Christian media, but we concluded the less distraction from the secular media the better, at least for the time being.

I, for one, wanted *no* media attention.

El mentioned, in passing, that after three *Donahue* sponsors withdrew we might want to call the local Christian radio station, KCBI, and inform them. (I couldn't envision three *Donahue* sponsors withdrawing. In fact, I couldn't envision even *one* withdrawing.)

El suggested that a friend of his might be able to get Nielsen ratings for us. He also brought up the name of Merrie Spaeth Lezar, whose company, Spaeth Communications, was to be immensely helpful in preparing me to face the media in the months to come.

Although I hadn't been involved in the campaign for a month yet, my emotional roller coaster ride had begun. I'd had several rough days during the two weeks before our lunch, but that gathering restored my feelings of hope and inspiration—at least for a while. Over the next months the phrase "ups and downs" was going to take on a whole new meaning for me.

Launching the Petition Drive

Monday, May 11, 1992. *Began circulating the petition. This kind of thing goes against my grain. I hope I'm the right man for this campaign. I guess the Lord thinks I am, whether I do or not.*

I would make a terrible insurance salesman. In fact, if I had to support myself as any kind of salesman, my family and I would probably starve. Nonetheless, here I was "selling" my campaign to the public!

My first step was to take the petitions to various churches, P.T.A. meetings, and civic groups. In her campaign Lynda distributed them to a number of other places, including doctors' offices. Fortunately, she was a capable representative of the campaign, because she had far more time available than I did. My friend David Miller, who is the director of the Tarrant County American Family Association, provided me with a list of 210 churches he felt would be interested in my efforts. I sent a postcard to each of those pastors, along with a sample petition, asking if they would circulate it. The results were surprisingly good.

DONAHUE UPDATE: AUGUST 4, 1992

Program subject: "Review of Nudity"—includes on-stage nudes and discussion of masturbation and intercourse.

Petition Regarding the Donahue Show

We, the undersigned, object to the viewing hour of the Donahue Show (WFAA-TV). This program is shown from 9-10 a.m. each weekday. At this time, especially during the summer vacation, there are many unsupervised children at home. Many of the topics on this show are not appropriate for children.

We request that this program be shown later, in the evening, when children are asleep.

Signature   Name Printed   Address Printed

_____   _____   _____

_____   _____   _____

_____   _____   _____

_____   _____   _____

_____   _____   _____

_____   _____   _____

_____   _____   _____

_____   _____   _____

Please return to: Richard Neill
                   P. O. Box 330128
                   Fort Worth, TX 76163

Probably 30 percent of those 210 churches responded. Many of them were small churches, with congregations of less than a hundred. But I was gratified; I had expected a response of only 3 to 5 percent. It was exciting to see churches and pastors who truly wanted to be "salt and light," churches that had chosen to take an uncompromising stand against evil.

As you launch your own petition, don't get discouraged if you are unable to gather a large number of signatures. I got thirteen thousand signatures on my petition; Lynda got eleven thousand on hers. I actually quit working on the petition drive after four thousand signatures, but by then the drive had its own momentum. Even if your signatures number in only the hundreds, remember the main reason you are gathering them—to raise community awareness and to let people know what you are trying to accomplish.

Seeking Christian Support

I knew it was important for me to rally support, so during this time I wrote my first letter to Concerned Women for America and sent it to Beverly LaHaye, the organization's president and founder. In fact, I sent more than one letter to her and didn't get a response for several weeks.

If you are launching a campaign similar to mine, keep in mind three key words:

Patience

Persistence

Perseverance

Those qualities are not innate in any of us. As I mentioned before, our "instant" society programs us to expect immediate responses. Whatever you do, keep at it. People in Christian leadership roles are extremely busy, and they receive tons of mail. Don't give up on them!

During this time, I also wrote to Focus on the Family and the local and state offices of the PTA. I called a number of church members in the Dallas/Fort Worth area. I followed lead after lead. Sometimes the results were positive, and sometimes they weren't.

Early in the campaign, I felt as if I were trying to push a locomotive down the track—I couldn't get it to budge. Several months down the road, the locomotive would be pushing me.

Why Donahue?

One pastor I met in early May was very supportive, but he asked a question which became extremely familiar before long: "Good idea. But why *Donahue?*"

First of all, *Phil Donahue* is the top-rated daytime television show in the Dallas/Fort Worth area, and he's among the top-rated daytime television shows in the country. He features the same sleazy material as Geraldo Rivera, Sally Jessy Raphael, and some of the other programs that struggle for ratings. But the truth is, Donahue doesn't need that kind of programming to keep his ratings up. Yet, he chooses to promote it anyway. Of all the talk shows, he has been around the longest and has become the leader that sets the standard for the others. As Debbie Price, a highly respected news columnist, once wrote, "If Phil Donahue interviews grandmothers who strip, how far will Maury Povich go?"

DONAHUE UPDATE: AUGUST 8, 1992

A divorced man talks about having sexual relations with his ex-wives.

Furthermore, Donahue's show happens to be the one I saw at the doctor's office, the one that caught my attention.

During those early days I was very moved when my mom called and offered to help circulate petitions. My mother, who is an optimist and an encourager, has always had a very positive influence on my life. There is no doubt that she and my father are to be credited with instilling in me the core of courage that sustained me throughout the campaign.

Tackling a Rock Concert

On May 15, Rhonda Shebek, one of my dental assistants, told me about a Christian heavy metal concert, which was to be held at a local high school gymnasium. A radio station had reported that the concert organizers were expecting two or three hundred people. My first thought was "Great! Two or three hundred signatures!"

If you had asked me a year before if I would be standing in the parking lot of a high school, trying to get the attention of teenagers on their way into a heavy metal concert, I would have laughed hysterically. I never dreamed I would do such a thing. But there we were—my wife, our two girls, and my eleven-year-old nephew, Jeremy.

When I called Cherry, my sister-in-law, to ask if Jeremy would like to go, she said, "Rick, I'm concerned about what you're doing. I'm afraid you're going to be vilified like you wouldn't believe." Although she was very much in favor of my campaign, she was concerned about the repercussions down the road. As it turned out, she was quite right—I was going to be vilified.

Some Surprising Responses

When you're taking a moral stand, it's one thing to be criticized and misunderstood by unbelievers. It's quite another to be criticized by fellow Christians. In early May, a friend of ours volunteered to do some legwork for me. When she returned, I asked, "Well, how did it go?"

She shook her head sadly, "I first went to the pastor of a Baptist church right down the street. When I told him about the campaign, I felt as if he were making fun of me. He said, 'What's wrong with Donahue? Why are you taking him on? I think he's a pretty good guy, and I like his programming.'"

Next, she had gone to a church where I had left petitions the week before. The pastor's secretary informed her, "This church operates a well-known Christian school in the area. The pastor is all for what you are doing. In fact, he really agrees with the stand you're taking, but he just doesn't feel we should get involved as a church."

Another friend, Dennis McClure, is on staff at a nearby church. Dennis introduced my campaign objectives at a staff meeting and said, "We should support Richard Neill. I know all about him, and he's a good guy." The pastor said, "No, that's a little bit too controversial for us. I don't want to get into that."

By the time I'd heard all that, the old emotional roller coaster was headed straight downhill. To make matters worse, Christi and I went to a social function at our church where a woman introduced herself to me and said, "You should take it easy on Phil. Phil and Geraldo are good guys. They've got decent programming. Really, the ones you should take on are Oprah and Sally Jessy Raphael. They're the ones with the terrible programming."

When Christi and I got home, we checked the video of that day's *Donahue* broadcast. A woman who had slept with her husband's brother was explaining how she felt when her young son walked in and found them in bed together.

So much for the "good" guy with "good" programming.

Three Important Questions

The next day, a dark cloud of discouragement hung over me. I felt heavy, weighed down with defeat, and I was beginning to see why Lynda emphasized and reemphasized prayer. Truly, a moral campaign is a spiritual and emotional battle.

From day one, the toughest part of the entire campaign has been the negative reactions of other Christians. One friend told me that Christians should only involve themselves in evangelism and discipleship. A woman told me, "I really don't want to circulate that petition because we don't have a TV set. We got rid of it when we got saved." A third friend, who meant well, said, "I'm so glad you're taking on *Donahue.*" I smiled and thanked him. Then he went on to say, "That should have been done a long time ago. And when you're through with him, I've got another one for you." He proceeded to name several other television programs he wanted *me* to get off the air. I thought, "If you only knew what's involved and how much work it takes. Why don't you do it yourself?"

I had to confess to the Lord that night, "Please forgive me for my wrong attitude toward all those people. Most of them are trying to do the right thing." That's one reason I'm writing this book. It's not enough for me to be involved. What about you? Here are some questions I hope you'll prayerfully consider.

- Do you believe Christian influence should go beyond evangelism?
- Do you agree that we have a responsibility to defend our nation's children from televised smut, even if we don't watch television ourselves?
- Do you feel that morality and political campaigns are always some other Christian's job?

Talk to your Christian friends. Read God's Word. Pray for His wisdom and direction. The task of confronting exploitative, sexually explicit television programming isn't the job of just one dentist from Texas. You may be just the person for the job in your home town.

Getting in Touch with Advertisers

Thursday, May 21, 1992. *Decided today that it's time to get in touch with local advertisers. This should heat things up....*

Lynda had spent six months circulating petitions in preparation for contacting Geraldo's advertisers. She and I decided I should spend three to six months doing the same thing. But things had progressed more quickly in my campaign, so I got the bright idea I should start contacting advertisers right away. I began with the top three local advertisers: Tom Thumb-Page Food Stores, The Cataract Institute of Texas, and The Carter Eye Center. These companies are located in the Dallas/Fort Worth area and aren't national chains or part of large, national or international corporations.

In a campaign, be sure you contact local advertisers first. These advertisers are far more susceptible to your influence since you are in their local market. You have a better chance of getting them to withdraw quickly than you'll have with an advertiser based halfway across the country, or a corporation that's advertising all across the country. Also, contact only one or two at a time, beginning with those that cater to families, such as food stores, car dealerships, and toy stores. Then you will be more likely to have some early successes.

This particular part of the campaign was especially intimidating to me. It bears repeating—I'm not a confrontational person. When I have to fire somebody at the office, I worry about it for weeks. Even after I decided to begin the battle with the advertisers it took awhile to prepare myself mentally for the conflict.

Help from the Home Church

Meanwhile, I realized I had never circulated my petition at our home church—Birchman Baptist Church in Fort Worth. Many people in my church are involved in the pro-life battle. Some are trying to improve public schools. Others are active in politics, in evangelizing the surrounding apartment complexes, or in feeding the poor—all as a result of the strong leadership and encouragement of our pastor, Miles Seaborn.

DONAHUE UPDATE: AUGUST 11, 1992

Program subjects: Sex with fathers, and oral sex.

One Sunday morning I took the "Dump Donahue" petition around to the various Sunday School rooms at my church, and when I returned to pick them up, page after page was full of signatures. I was elated! I praised God for every signature and prayed He would remind me of this bright moment of encouragement the next time spiritual darkness began to surround me.

As I sat in the quietness of the sanctuary, waiting for the worship service to begin, I read Acts 4:13: "When they saw the courage of Peter and John and realized that they were unschooled, ordinary men, they were astonished and they took note that these men had been with Jesus."

I began to think about the boldness of Peter and John and about the persecution of the early church members. They were hated and despised. They were challenged and confronted. They were willing to lay their lives on the line for Christ. "No matter how tough it gets," I told myself, "Christians today don't have to face the kind of challenges the early church did.

"Lord," I silent prayed, "when all this is said and done, please let everyone be astonished by what You have done. And make it clear to everyone that, just like Peter and John, I have been with Jesus, too."

CHAPTER FIVE

Pulling on the Purse Strings

June 4, 1992. Called the CEO of Tom Thumb-Page Food Stores. Conversation was surprisingly easy. Campaign is at a new stage now that I'm contacting local advertisers.

Although it was clearly time to move forward and contact some of Donahue's local advertisers, I was nervous about actually picking up the phone and calling Tom Thumb. I summoned all my courage and said, "This is Dr. Richard Neill, and I would like to speak with Jack Evans." Mr. Evans was the president of Tom Thumb-Page at that time.

"May I ask what this is in regard to?" the secretary asked.

"It's in regard to Tom Thumb's advertising practices."

When she connected me with Mr. Evans, I could hardly believe it. Like a lot of other things that happened at the beginning of the campaign, I can see now that the Lord was making my way much easier than it might have been.

I told Mr. Evans I had been monitoring the *Donahue* program and explained that some of the broadcasts' content was extremely objectionable. "I've done some research," I explained. "Would you mind taking a look at it and reconsidering your sponsorship of the program? I'm also asking some other companies to pull out."

He was very gracious. "Yes," he said, "I would be happy to look at it. I can't make a decision right now, but if the material we're sponsoring is pretty bad stuff, we don't want to be a part of it." Although he didn't make any commitments, I could tell he was a man of strong character and willing to consider a change.

I was ecstatic! I felt as if I had conquered the world. All morning long I thought, "This campaign is going to work!"

Encouraging Words from Local Sponsors

Motivated by my success, I made another call that day to Dr. Harvey Carter, the owner of Carter Eye Centers in Dallas. Since he was unavailable, I decided to send him a letter.

I also called Dr. James Bentley, the owner of the Cataract Institute of Texas, a Dallas business which sponsored *Donahue*. I said, "This is Dr. Richard Neill, and I would like to schedule an appointment to speak with Dr. Bentley when he's finished seeing his patients. It won't take thirty minutes of his time."

"When would you like to schedule that time?" the secretary asked.

"Tomorrow if possible."

"Fine."

Fine? Again it seemed as if the Lord was opening these doors with little help from me. Most corporations don't just say, "Yes, come on over" the first time somebody calls. Generally you have to call repeatedly.

After I made the phone call, I sat there thinking, "Is this really what I want to get into?" Then I called our friend Ronnie Mosley and asked if he would like to go to Dallas with Christi and me. I invited them to join me, because Lynda Beams had suggested having witnesses in any interview or meeting. Besides, I needed moral support.

I was anxious about the meeting, preferring to make my requests by letter or phone. Actually, most of the appeals in such a campaign are by letter. You can't possibly make enough phone calls to reach everyone, and you aren't able to visit many sponsors in person because of their location.

That evening I spent a great deal of time in prayer, asking the Lord again, "Is this really what you want me to do? I feel as if you've called me to do this job, and I'm proceeding with it. So I pray that you'll bless my obedience. I pray that you'll give us confidence when we go into

June 2, 1992

Dr. Harvey Carter
Carter Eye Center
3310 Live Oak
Dallas, TX 75204

Dear Dr. Carter:

I can honestly say I am as offended as I have ever been over a daytime television program.

I will never forget the sickening feeling I had recently while sitting in the waiting room of my doctor's office with my five-year-old daughter. Several children hovered around a television set in the room and watched as Phil Donahue stood before a panel of three mother-child teams in his New York studio. This began a live program entitled "My Mother Is a Slut" in which one mother, Sabrina Asset, claimed to have had sex with 2,759 men.

While waiting for my appointment, I began to wonder: Is this kind of explicit programming a regular occurrence on *Donahue*? After ordering 120 transcripts and taping *Donahue* programs for twelve months, I was shocked to find that there is a regular pattern of disgusting, sleazy topics on *Donahue*. A very small sample of the topics of discussion included: mother-daughter stripper teams; penis transplants and managing erections; mutual masturbation and incest; a man in his third marriage who sleeps only with his first two wives; a sadomasochist mistress with a dungeon and sex slaves; group sex and locker room gang rape; and religious, ritualistic sex with more than one partner at a time. All this from the show with the current ad slogan "All kinds of people...like you."

When I learned that Carter Eye Center is one of the sponsors, I was shocked. I am well aware of your excellent reputation as a leader in the com-

munity. You still have my utmost respect. I can
only assume you are unaware of the type of programming you are sponsoring.

The Nielsen Television Ratings state that there
are thousands of children that watch *Donahue* daily
in the Dallas/Fort Worth area. Almost a half-mil-
lion kids watch this program each day on a
national basis.

The support from other parents has been overwhelming. I have received several thousand signatures
on petitions within just a few weeks. This is
definitely a community concern.

I taped several *Donahue* shows and condensed them
into a twenty-one-minute video, which will be
mailed to your office. I have enclosed a compilation of excerpts of some of Phil Donahue's recent
productions.

My campaign has the support of several local organizations, including the Dallas Association for
Decency and the American Family Association.

I am requesting that you discontinue your commercials on *Donahue*, and I am asking that you
respond to this request by June 14, 1992.

Sincerely,

Richard B. Neill

that meeting tomorrow and that you will already be working on the heart of this gentleman."

As we approached Dr. Bentley's office, I was getting more anxious by the minute. We drove into the parking lot about twenty minutes early so we could spend time in prayer before going inside. We prayed that God would give us wisdom and clarity of thought, and we asked Him to prepare Dr. Bentley's heart.

Despite all that, before we walked in, I looked over at Ronnie and Christi and said, "You know what? I don't want to do this!"

DONAHUE UPDATE: AUGUST 13, 1992

Two gays describe having sex with a lesbian on the same night so she wouldn't know which one fathered her baby.

When we arrived, a staff meeting was in progress, so we waited about half an hour. Of course the wait did my nervousness no good at all. However, when Dr. Bentley finally came in, it was immediately evident that he was an approachable man.

After a few minutes of small talk, I said, "I know you're busy and I won't keep you long, but we are here to discuss some questionable television programming." I went on to explain that the *Donahue* program was becoming more and more sexually explicit with recent broadcasts on sex change operations, lesbian wedding ceremonies, strippers, a school cafeteria worker having sex with an elementary school child, and a high school teacher taking students home to have sex with him. "What concerns me most," I concluded, "is that children are able to flip on the television set and watch that stuff. The Cataract Institute of Texas is one of the top three local sponsors. Would you consider withdrawing your advertising?" With that, I handed him my three-page report.

After skimming the report briefly, Dr. Bentley said, "I think you're right." There was a pause. "We're going to withdraw by Monday." He hadn't given it five minutes' thought! "*Donahue* is a big draw for us. It's a top-rated program. But, you're right—I don't think we need our name associated with this material."

I managed to look professional and keep my emotions in check, but on the inside, I was jumping up and down with excitement. We talked for another thirty minutes, and he gave us a tour of the office. But once we left the building and were out of sight, I shouted for joy. What a victory God had given us! As we drove home, it was as if the wheels of the car never touched the ground. This was the first real victory in the campaign, and God had shown Himself very powerful indeed.

Saturday, June 6, 1992. *God has given me such a sense of boldness after the meeting in Dallas that I'm eager to write some of the other companies.*

By this point I had received eighteen hundred signatures on petitions, and many people were expressing a desire to get involved in the campaign. I was profoundly encouraged—so much so that I worked until eleven that night writing letters to several other advertisers, six months ahead of plan. I wrote to Foley's Department Stores, Albertson's, a regional food store chain, and Food Lion, another grocery store chain. Although they are not huge national corporations, they are major advertisers on a local and regional basis.

An important tip in contacting a large corporation is to write to the top three executives in the company: the CEO, the president of the company, and the vice president of marketing or advertising. In some companies, the CEO is also the president. If so, try to get two other names. Chances are, at some point the executives will get together and say, "Did you get the same thing in the mail about the *Donahue* program that I did?"

June 6, 1992

Mr. John Carley, President
Albertson's
250 Park Center Blvd.
Boise, ID 83726

Dear Mr. Carley:

For several years, I have been concerned about
television programming and its effects on children. After viewing several *Donahue* programs in
which he and guests discussed such disgusting topics as teenage transsexuals, a sadomasochist mistress with a dungeon and sex slaves, mutual masturbation, mother-daughter stripper teams, managing erections, and group sex parties, I determined
he had crossed the line into extreme obscenity. I
decided I could no longer remain silent and that
I must use my influence to make a difference.

As a result, I have begun a campaign to protect
children from this type of destructive influence,
and the support from other parents has been overwhelming. In several weeks, I have received almost
two thousand signatures on petitions. New groups
are daily requesting petitions to sign.

The PTAs across the country are enthusiastically
pursuing an end to the sexually explicit tabloid
shows such as *Donahue*. PTAs in our country are
extremely influential.

I taped several *Donahue* programs to see what is
available for children to view on a consistent
basis. When I learned that you are an advertiser
on *Donahue*, I was shocked and bitterly disappointed,
since I felt that your company was associated with
quality and a wholesomeness uniquely associated
with Americans and their families. You have such
an excellent reputation. I can only assume that
you are unaware of the content of the more recent
Donahue shows.

I have condensed several *Donahue* programs into a twenty-one-minute video. A sample of the excerpts of programs produced recently are:

1) A young girl has oral sex and intercourse with her father in front of her brother who is having sex with the mother.
2) A mother picks up her teenage daughter's boyfriend from school, takes him home, and has an affair with him.
3) A married couple discusses the possibilities of having other people over for dinner and sex. One person says, "My husband gave me permission to have sex with other men as an anniversary present."
4) Explicit details of a three-year-old child performing oral sex on his mother. Erections and intercourse with the mother are also discussed.
5) A woman discusses her role as the high priestess of sex in the "Church of the Most High Goddess," where sex is sacred. She says, "I have sex for religious purposes, to purify people." She has had this purification ritual with 2,759 church members. Another guest says she like to have sex with more than one person at a time.
6) Discussion of a boss masturbating in front of his secretary.
7) A male stripper bragging about his sexual conquests of over 2,000 women, sometimes several at the same time.

The video is available to you. I have enclosed a compilation of excerpts of some of Phil Donahue's productions since January 1, 1992. I am embarrassed to mail this since it is so disgusting and saddening to me.

At the present time, two of the top local Donahue sponsors have withdrawn all commercial support of *Donahue*. I have received no refusals.

I realize you may not wish to be labeled as a sponsor, and the definition of the word is not important. You advertise on *Donahue*, a show that frequently promotes what many consider to be soft-core pornography and which undermines traditional family values. Regardless of the type of advertising plan (ROS, etc.), when you advertise within a program you are helping support it and are identified with that program.

I have rallied the support of a number of national organizations and coalitions, most of which have memberships of several million. The following are just a few of the organizations which are standing beside me and have supported this effort: Concerned Women for America, the Dallas Association for Decency, Morality in Media, the Southern Baptist Convention, Focus on the Family, Eagle Forum, the Christian Coalition, the Family Research Council, the PTA, and the American Family Association.

I am urgently appealing to you for your help and am requesting that you discontinue your commercials on *Donahue* in every state in which you advertise. I am asking that you respond to this request by June 16, 1992.

Sincerely,

Dr. Richard B. Neill

(Note to the reader: Later in the campaign, I might list twenty to twenty-five company names that had withdrawn support, for added influence.)

Monday, June 9, 1992. *I called the president of Buy Owner Real Estate, Brandon Baker. Another friendly conversation. Also called Laser Surgery Associates and wrote another letter to WFAA.*

As Mr. Baker and I talked, I expressed my concern about the *Donahue* program and the fact that his company was helping pay for it.

"Send me the information as quickly as you can," he responded. "I'll look over it in the next couple of days and get back with you."

I sent the information, fully expecting to hear from him in the next couple of days.

I didn't.

When I called one of the other large local sponsors, Laser Surgery Associates, I spoke to one of the doctors personally. "I'm calling because I'm concerned about your advertising on the *Donahue* program. And I wanted to speak with you about that if I could," I said.

"Let me call you back," he responded.

"That's fine. When would be a good time?"

"I don't know. Let *me* call *you* back," he said nervously. Then he hung up on me.

The same day I wrote another letter to WFAA's general manager, David Lane, again requesting that they move *Donahue* to a time slot after eleven at night.

More Ups and Downs along the Way

Just as I was beginning to feel fatigued and discouraged again, there came another great victory. Mr. Evans at Tom Thumb-Page Food Stores wrote to say his sponsorship of *Donahue* was definitely over. Praise God for His power!

Buoyed by this success, on June 17 I sent off my second letter to the advertisers who had not responded to my first one.

On June 18, 1992, David Lane, president and general manager of WFAA, responded by letter, claiming that the station had pulled those *Donahue* programs that were adult-oriented. I knew that wasn't quite accurate. The good news was, he said they had pulled three sexually explicit programs off the air over the past six months. The bad news was, they had aired about thirty others!

On June 19, Carter Eye Center and Food Lion dropped *Donahue.* The president of Food Lion told me by phone, "We're pulling out immediately, no problem. I agree with you 100 percent." Four sponsors had now dropped out.

Meanwhile, I was receiving letters back from other sponsors. Over the course of the campaign, I have been encouraged by the response of so many companies.

How Advertisers Sometimes Respond

If you're putting together a campaign to fight smut on television, you'll eventually have to write the sponsors. Here are the six most typical responses you can expect to receive from advertisers.

RESPONSE #1:

"We're pulling out immediately." You'll be surprised that a few advertisers will respond after a single letter, or sometimes just two or three. In my case, these were form letters which were modified slightly for each company.

RESPONSE #2:

"You've made a mistake. We don't advertise on that show." There won't be any mistake if you've kept good records. Go back and check again. Then send them some type of documentation. I've even offered to send them a tape of the program with their advertisement on it. That always settles the matter.

RESPONSE #3:

"We stay off the bad broadcasts and advertise only on the good ones." If you receive a response that says, "Thank you for your letter, but we monitor *Donahue,* and we're going to stay off of the sexually explicit programs," then you'll have to document any sexually explicit programs they advertise on after the date of their letter. Once you have documentation, send them another letter that says, "I appreciate your remarks, but unfortunately your philosophy is in direct contradiction to your actions. I would appreciate your response to that contradiction because you are still sponsoring sexually explicit programs."

RESPONSE #4:

"We have no control over where our advertisement shows up." This is not totally accurate. There is an agreement, called a "run of station" or ROS agreement, that advertisers can buy. They buy into a certain period of time, for example between eight in the morning and noon, and the station can put their advertisement anywhere they wish within that time frame.

However, let these advertisers know they can stipulate that they want to avoid the *Donahue* program, or the *Geraldo* program, or whatever program is objectionable even though they are buying a certain time period. They will claim they cannot, but they can. Stand your ground and hold them accountable. Dozens of corporations have stipulated they want to avoid *Donahue* even though they have an ROS agreement.

DONAHUE UPDATE: AUGUST 17, 1992

Parents explain why they allow their children to have sex at home.

RESPONSE #5:

"Give us some time to check into it—we'll get back to you." Advertisers may stall, hoping if they put you off long enough you'll not write again. Remember, corporate advertisers are used to hearing from viewers who are angry about a program or a product—viewers who send one letter, get the problem out of their systems, and never contact them again.

Here, persistence is the key. Once they realize you aren't going to give up, they'll start paying attention.

RESPONSE #6:

"Thank you for your concern. We do try to monitor the programs, and we'll try to do better." Don't assume this is the end of it. Again, these advertisers know that most people who complain will write only once.

Simple solution: keep watching and, if the ads continue, keep writing. Say, "Thanks for pledging to do better, but my question is still unanswered: "Will your company pull its advertising support from the *Donahue* show?"

RESPONSE #7:

"We're sorry we offended you, but we're going to continue to advertise." Some of the advertisers I wrote to were totally unyielding, but they were few and far between. However, even the majority of these will eventually listen, especially to the financial impact they will eventually face. You will be able to put a great deal of pressure on them.

Take Advertisers at Their Word

I'm convinced that many of the executives with corporate advertisers are family people, just like you and me. They are at such a high rung on the corporate ladder that they have passed on these decisions to an advertising department within the company, or to an outside advertising agency.

Most companies buy their advertising slots by the ratings, and they want to be on programs that have large audiences. They don't even look at content. So when companies write back and say they didn't realize what subject matter was on the program, I take their word for it.

If the executive is genuinely concerned, he will withdraw his sponsorship. If he is simply putting you off, you'll have to stay after him. As I've already noted, a few companies require only one letter to withdraw. In other cases, I have seen companies require twenty-five to thirty letters to each top executive in the company. Multiply that by the three top executives, and it may require sending seventy-five letters before a company withdraws.

You also have to realize that you could send some companies letters from now till the end of time, and they would never withdraw. However, that's the exception. Ninety percent of companies are concerned about keeping family-oriented people as consumers. They don't want to take the chance of losing this customer base.

When writing to sponsors, mention any large organizations which are in agreement with what you're doing and the number of people involved with these organizations. For example, once Concerned Women for America gave me permission to use their name, I mentioned in some of my letters that they were in agreement with my campaign and that they have over 600,000 members. The advertiser can immediately envision 600,000 lost consumers.

More Good News from Sponsors

On June 22, Blackmon-Mooring-Steamatic, a small advertiser that only bought a few advertising spots, withdrew from *Donahue*. That same day, the president of Albertson's wrote to say that his corporation had put *Donahue* on their "programs to avoid" list years before. Somehow it had since slipped through the cracks. He promised they would stop sponsoring *Donahue* immediately.

Things were going so well I decided it was time to let the Christian media know about it.

Taking the Plunge into Christian Media

I decided to call a national radio network based in Dallas called the USA Radio Network. I told the man who answered, "I don't know whom I need to speak to. I've got a campaign going against the *Donahue* program."

He asked some questions, and I mentioned some of the subject matter Donahue was exploiting. "Yeah, that does sound pretty bad," he remarked. "Let me put you in contact with John Clemens. Can you hold the line?"

John Clemens is the news director for the USA Radio Network, which at that time went out over 935 stations, nationwide. It's even bigger now.

I explained my mission to John Clemens and told him about the tactics I was using. I said, "I don't think this is news right now, but I wanted to let you know what was going on and that five of Phil Donahue's biggest advertisers in this market have withdrawn their advertising completely from his show."

DONAHUE UPDATE: AUGUST 18, 1992

Program subject: "Bisexual sex practices."

"Not news?" he shouted. "That's big news! And I'd like to do a story immediately."

"Well, it doesn't seem like news to me." By then, I was trying to get out of it.

"Oh yeah, it's definitely big news. Do you have time to do an interview right now?"

I choked. "Well, I guess so."

And so he interviewed me right there on the phone, knocking knees and all.

I thought I would be the only one involved in the interview, but then he interviewed David Lane, the president of WFAA, the ABC affiliate that carried the program in Dallas. And, to make matters worse (or so it seemed to me), he also interviewed a public relations representative for the *Donahue* show in New York.

I was in utter shock. "I can't believe I did that!" I chastised myself. "This is going out to several million people, and my campaign isn't going to be a secret any longer. And on top of that, they just interviewed the *Donahue* show and channel 8 in Dallas. What have I done?"

John Clemens informed me that the program would air on June 26. I thanked him and hung up, and then my wheels immediately started turning: "How can I make the most of this? Several stubborn sponsors have been ignoring me. I need to use this somehow to get them to wake up and pull their advertising."

Making the Most of the Media

I composed the letter on the following page. Notice I didn't say I was calling for a boycott. I didn't threaten them in any way. But I did let them know this interview was going to be broadcast nationwide. That's all they needed to know—I left the rest up to their imagination. I sent those four letters out by Federal Express on June 23 and was so excited that night I slept only four hours.

Keep this in mind if you're involved in a campaign. When there is going to be a newspaper article or a radio or television interview on the campaign, write the sponsors and let them know. I suggest you don't mention boycotts until the sponsors have received a number of letters. But always let advertisers know when you're going to get public attention and when they might get public attention if they choose to continue their association with a particular program.

June 26, 1992. *The USA Radio interview. Another major breakthrough for the campaign. And three more sponsors dropped* Donahue *today. Exciting day!*

Before the USA program aired that morning, I received responses from three of the four stubborn companies, notifying me they would be withdrawing immediately.

Two were very polite: "Thank you for your concern for America's children. We're going to be pulling out our *Donahue* sponsorship immediately."

The third response came as a telephone call from an angry department store vice president. I could tell I was on a speaker phone in her

June 22, 1992

Mr. Alex Dillard, President
Dillard's Department Stores
1600 Cantrell Road
Little Rock, AR 72201

Dear Mr. Dillard:

I have recently sent you several letters and a
packet of information concerning your advertising
on the *Donahue Show*. I still have not received a
response from you.

Recent topics and discussions on *Donahue* include:

* A man, who dresses as a woman, discusses how he
  talks like a woman. He says, "I'm so horny and
  so wet."
* A woman pulls down her bra during the program.
* Women who love sex addicts. Includes discussion
  of masturbation.
* Guests include homosexual and bisexual males
  and females. They discuss two homosexuals
  "rubbing each other's penises on the beach."

On June 26, 1992, I will give Mr. John Clemens of
the USA Radio Network an update on my campaign.
The USA Radio Network airs on 965 radio stations
nationwide. I will be furnishing him with a list
of topics from the program, sponsors who are withdrawing, and name of any company that has refused.

Once again, I am requesting that you withdraw your
company's commercials from *Donahue*. Unless I
receive a response from you by June 26, 1992, I
will assume that you wish to continue your support
of the *Donahue Show*.

Sincerely,

Richard B. Neill

office, and I could envision several executives sitting around listening to the conversation. She began rather sarcastically, "We can tell you've spent a lot of time on this campaign. What is it you want us to do, Dr. Neill?"

I responded as nondefensively as possible, "Well, what I'm asking you to do is to help protect children from watching the *Phil Donahue* program. Would you withdraw your advertisements from his show?"

She explained, "Well, there's no decision to be made, because we withdrew from them yesterday, by coincidence. You had nothing to do with our decision."

"Great!" I was genuinely pleased. "I appreciate your doing that. Would you mind sending me a letter as confirmation?"

"No, Dr. Neill, you won't be getting any letter. That's not necessary. We don't want you mentioning our company's name in any way. We made a decision, totally without regard to you or any of your letters."

"That's quite a coincidence," I thought. "They've been advertising on *Donahue* for about four years, and it just so happens they've withdrawn one day after my last letter went out. But I'll take it any way I can get it."

I was ecstatic.

"We're Going to Sue You!"

Despite these successes, my fourth letter drew fire. The fourth advertiser, the one who did not withdraw, wrote a letter threatening a lawsuit. In fact, I have been threatened with lawsuits five times over the last year and a half. At first, that was a big concern to me because I didn't want to lose everything I owned. As it turned out, I had nothing to fear. I've learned you don't need to worry about a lawsuit if:

1. you are truthful in your excerpts from the show in question;
2. you are accurate in your documentation of the days the company advertised on the program;

3. you don't employ name-calling;
4. you do not allow yourself to become emotional.

There's no reason to be alarmed about lawsuits. First of all, a major television production company is not going to sue you because you're just a little guy. It would be terrible public relations for the media to learn, for example, that Phil Donahue is suing Richard Neill, or Geraldo is suing Lynda Beams. People in power know that.

Also, a large corporation doesn't want bad publicity, especially when an individual is trying to protect children. That would be the worst possible advertising they could get. They simply are not going to go after you. As long as you are truthful and honest, and as long as you are prayed up and God is in the battle, be at peace. You are going to be protected—physically, financially, and spiritually.

LEGAL INFORMATION

1. *Always be completely truthful and accurate in your statements to sponsors, media, producers or anyone else involved. Don't exaggerate, and don't guess if you are not absolutely certain about the facts. Keep accurate records, including dates.*

2. *Do not personally attack a producer, a sponsor, or a program host. Attack only the issue: sleaze programming.*

3. *Don't be fearful of lawsuits from advertisers, television stations, or program executives. They know the bad publicity would hurt them a lot more than it could hurt you.*

4. *Position yourself as the little guy—a nobody—so the opposition isn't tempted to go after you. Organizations that supported me were threatened with lawsuits more than I was.*

5. *Bear in mind that you are simply exercising your first amendment right to free speech.*

6. *Remember that spiritual warfare is a part of any moral campaign and that the enemy employs fear as a tactic. He will try to use your fear of a lawsuit to immobilize you.*

7. *Call the legal center at the American Family Association in Tupelo, Mississippi, if you have legal questions or concerns. Even before you begin your campaign, you may want to call and confer with their experts.*

CHAPTER SIX

The Battle Heats Up

F ollowing the broadcast of John Clemens' interview, literally hundreds of letters arrived at my mailbox—all but three or four of which were wonderfully encouraging and supportive. I was humbled to realize that so many people cared about what I was doing.

At the beginning of the campaign, I had rented a box at the local post office, and I would suggest you do the same if you take on a campaign. For your safety and peace of mind it's important not to give out your home address.

Personal peace of mind is always a precious commodity, and particularly so in the midst of a moral or political campaign. Although the Lord has promised us "the peace that passes understanding," if you're like me, you will have some emotional turmoil along the way. For example, after the USA Radio Network broadcast, Christi and I were troubled that a representative from the *Donahue* show had been interviewed, as well as the president of WFAA. The "secret" had been revealed. The proverbial cat was out of the bag.

It's amazing how we can second-guess ourselves. Initially, I had felt God's guidance when I called the USA Radio Network, which is one of the biggest Christian media outlets available. By now, I was seriously doubting that decision. In fact, I had basically decided I had done the wrong thing. I dreaded the scrutiny and possible attacks on my character that my new visibility might provoke.

But just about the time I began to feel depressed about the unpleasant possibilities, good things began to happen again.

Taking Another Bold Step

June 29, 1992. *Received word today that the tenth* Donahue *sponsor has pulled out. Great news!*

Hearing about the tenth advertiser's decision to drop *Donahue* reconfirmed my faith in the campaign and in the fact that God was really guiding me. So I decided to take another step: I sent letters to the top twenty national advertisers.

The national advertisers are in a totally different league from the local and regional ones I had written to earlier. These are huge companies with multimillion dollar advertising accounts—Kraft General Foods, American Home Products, Sara Lee Corporation, Kmart Corporation, SC Johnson Wax, Warner Lambert, Lever Brothers, Clorox Company, Marshall's Department Stores, Baskin-Robbins, to name a few.

Secretly I had visions that within a week or two they would all raise white flags and say, "You win! We give up, and we're going to pull out all our advertising across the country." Reality is, national advertisers are much tougher to deal with than the local ones. Fortunately, the Lord had given me my initial boldness, or I would have been much more hesitant to start this new process.

I sent all those letters by certified mail, because I wanted to make an impact on the corporate executives. But if I had it to do over again, I probably would send the letters by regular mail. Certified is expensive, and in my experience regular mail does the job just as well.

July 1, 1992. *I received an encouraging letter from Morris Jarvis, the CEO of Hancock Fabrics.*

The letter from this Christian executive typifies the support I received from many sponsors. His response was especially meaningful to me:

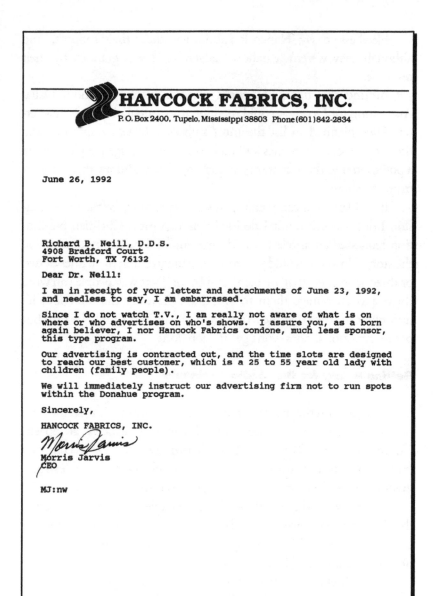

HANCOCK FABRICS, INC.
P. O. Box 2400, Tupelo, Mississippi 38803   Phone (601) 842-2834

June 26, 1992

Richard B. Neill, D.D.S.
4908 Bradford Court
Fort Worth, TX 76132

Dear Dr. Neill:

I am in receipt of your letter and attachments of June 23, 1992, and needless to say, I am embarrassed.

Since I do not watch T.V., I am really not aware of what is on where or who advertises on who's shows. I assure you, as a born again believer, I nor Hancock Fabrics condone, much less sponsor, this type program.

Our advertising is contracted out, and the time slots are designed to reach our best customer, which is a 25 to 55 year old lady with children (family people).

We will immediately instruct our advertising firm not to run spots within the Donahue program.

Sincerely,

HANCOCK FABRICS, INC.

Morris Jarvis
CEO

MJ:nw

Hancock Fabrics - Minnesota Fabrics - Fabric Warehouse - Fabric Market

Needless to say, Hancock Fabrics withdrew their support. And although they weren't a national advertiser, I was gratified by their response.

Around this time, El Arnold asked if his organization, Dallas Association for Decency, could mention my campaign in their newsletter. They planned to list the most stubborn *Donahue* sponsors and their top executives' names and addresses to encourage people to write a polite letter to those sponsors, requesting they withdraw their support from the show.

If you launch a campaign, you may want to make the same decision I did—at this point I decided that anytime a Christian publication requested an article I would say, "Sure, I'll be happy to give you the story. However, would you mind my mentioning the names of two or three advertisers that are being stubborn? That way people can write them and encourage them to withdraw." During the interview, it's important to stress that the letters to the advertisers should be firm but polite. Emotional ones won't get the job done.

Getting Ready for the Media Onslaught

Dealing with the media remained my number one fear, so the time had come for me to meet with Melinda Matthews at Spaeth Communications. Owned by Merrie Spaeth Lezar, this Dallas company trains people to deal with the media. Although there is some expense involved, they are topnotch, and I highly recommend them.

When I walked in the door of the attractive, woodframe structure that houses their offices, I was thinking, "There's absolutely no way I can handle the media, especially the secular media." As I left the session, I was thinking, "I can do this! I actually can do this!"

When Melinda and I sat down in Merrie Lezar's office, I glanced at the impressive surroundings. There were pictures of her with other people she has helped—people like George Bush and Ronald Reagan! In fact, she was a member of Reagan's White House staff.

If you're going to have a campaign, I can assure you that you will be dealing with the media, whether you like it or not. With that in mind, let me share with you some of the invaluable strategy I have learned, especially from Spaeth Communications.

DEALING WITH THE FRIENDLY PRESS

1. **Rapport:** *Establish a friendly, personal relationship with media personnel. Make them aware of who you are and of your availability. Don't assume they know all about you and what you're doing.*

2. **Publicity:** *Always inform them of anything relevant to your campaign. Never assume they will automatically know about news items or upcoming events. If you are dealing with print media, try to determine what format they prefer for press releases.*

3. **Patience:** *Remember that they have busy schedules, a broad spectrum of concerns, and probably a large area to cover. Don't be discouraged if they don't treat your news with the priority or enthusiasm you would like.*

DEALING WITH THE HOSTILE PRESS

1. **Tact:** *Always remain tactful and courteous with the media, whether on camera, in print, or privately.*

2. **Don't react.** *Your opposition may attack you or your motives. They may try to divert attention away from your primary concerns and focus on secondary issues. But never react to your opposition. Ignore them and focus on the issues; always stay on the issues. The media loves to project conflict and will attempt to cause reaction between opposing viewpoints, sharing with each side the other's response.*

3. **Format Strategy:** *Decide what kinds of appearances you will make and what type of interviews you will give. In my campaign, I avoided all talk show formats where there was a live audience and a panel. In other words, I would not go on* Donahue, *or* Oprah, *or* Geraldo— *any of the television talk shows.*

   However, I did not avoid radio talk shows. I did all of those. I also gave every interview that the print media asked me for, with the exception of the tabloid newspapers, such as the Star *and the* National

Enquirer. *Don't feel like you have to give an interview to everybody that calls. Just be well prepared when you do grant an interview.*

4. **Debate:** *My advice is to avoid debate formats. I've found that very little is accomplished in debating our issues in secular media. The host is usually prejudiced, and very few hosts will be open-minded enough to allow your viewpoint full and fair consideration.*

5. **Positivism:** *Don't be discouraged if you don't do well in an interview. There will be many other opportunities, as long as you don't give up. Experience will quickly teach you how to use the media to your advantage.*

One Crisis after Another

July 9, 1992. *If anything can go wrong, it's going wrong right now. Problems at work. Trouble at home. Christi and I have to talk or we're going to have a major crisis.*

Many people have asked me what kind of an impact the campaign had on my work and my family. First of all, I have to say that without my wife Christi the campaign never would have happened. I'd also have to say that, despite all her support and encouragement, it wasn't easy—not at all.

Running a dental practice is certainly a major responsibility in the best of times. Running a dental practice and a moral campaign at the same time is an unbelievable undertaking. The campaign itself could easily be a full-time job. As a matter of fact, if you are considering a campaign like mine, I want to assure you that it's a fulfilling endeavor; however, it would be wise to have three or four other people in a coalition with you to spread out the responsibilities.

Just to give you an idea of what life during a campaign may be like, let me tell you what happened to us during early July of 1992.

My dental office sends crowns and bridges and other lab work to various dental laboratories by UPS mail. One of the dental labs I use is out of state—I continue to do business with them because they do excellent work. In twelve years of practice we had never had a problem. But in one week of July, thirteen of our lab cases, involving thirteen different patients, were lost.

To this day I don't know what happened to them. The lab said they never received them, although I know we sent them. We tried to resolve the problem in every conceivable way, but when all was said and done, it felt like a spiritual problem—the enemy seemed to be trying to totally discourage me. If that's what he was up to, he was being pretty successful. And he wasn't finished, either.

DONAHUE UPDATE: AUGUST 21, 1992

Program title: "The Sex Shop."

July 9 had to be the longest day of the year. On that day one of my best secretaries, who had been with me for about three years, informed me she was going to quit and stay home with her children. That very same day another secretary, who had been with me four years, also gave notice. She was probably one of the three best employees I've ever had.

When I got home, after having three major crises at work, Christi said, "This is not going to work. You either have to back off, prioritize things and get a life again, or I don't think you should be involved in this campaign. You can't keep ignoring your family and ruining your health by not getting enough sleep. This is ridiculous!"

Until that time I had poured nearly every ounce of energy I had into the campaign. Christi had been supportive, but for months she had seen me go into the study and shut the door, not to emerge again until bedtime. Now she'd had enough. Naturally, I knew that isolating myself like that wasn't right, but I hadn't changed my routine.

At first I wasn't receptive to what she had to say. I was wrung out and feeling a lot of stress from the office situation. We must have talked for three hours about it, and both of us were emotionally at the end of our rope. I didn't want to give up the campaign, but we decided to pray that God would bring along some other people to help.

New Resolutions

I resolved to come home every day at five o'clock and spend from five to eight in the evening with my family. Once Christi and I got the children to bed at eight o'clock, I would go in and work on the Donahue project. And that's what I did for the rest of the campaign. Christi and I also made arrangements to spend time together as a couple without the children.

In addition, I decided to take off early on Wednesdays and Thursdays, at least while the campaign was going. We moved our girls to a Christian school across the street from my office, and every Wednesday I took Lauri Ann on an after-school date. I did the same with Natalie on Thursdays. We'd go bowling. We'd go out for pizza or Mexican food. Or we'd go to a movie or to a museum. This has been a delightful addition to our lives.

With or without the campaign, this turned out to be a great turning point for our family. I had to wake up and face the fact that our three children weren't going to be young much longer. I was reminded that my primary motivation for the campaign was for my kids and that my family is much more important to me than taking on the *Phil Donahue Show.*

Although I made the decision to prioritize my life more intelligently in the middle of the campaign, I encourage you to get your priorities straight at the very beginning. Count on a heavy investment of time for your efforts, but don't let it rob your family. Find another place to cut back.

Words of Wisdom

Not only did my wife have some important words for me, I also began to listen more carefully to God after that nightmarish day in July. I remember reading about the suffering of Jesus in 1 Peter 2:24: "He himself bore our sins in his body on the tree, so that we might die to sins and live for righteousness; by his wounds you have been healed."

And I read in Mark 10 the story of Zebedee's sons, who wanted to sit on either side of Jesus in heaven. Jesus' disciples were always wanting to share His glory. He pointedly asked them, "Are you willing to drink from the cup that I drink from? Are you willing to suffer?"

They, of course, responded enthusiastically, "Yes." But I don't think they knew what they were saying. I certainly hadn't known at the beginning of my campaign when I had said I was willing to "suffer for God."

How we Christians yearn for "feel good" doctrine and wholeheartedly embrace the "feel good" theology that is preached in many pulpits. We're so enthusiastic about feeling good that we forget altogether about the matter of suffering. Yet suffering is a principle Christ taught over and over again—in the Christian life, distress will occur. The Bible actually says we should welcome it: "Consider it pure joy, my brothers, whenever you face trials of many kinds, because you know that the testing of your faith develops perseverance. Perseverance must finish its work so that you may be mature and complete, not lacking anything" (James 1:2-4).

On July 9, 1992, I wasn't considering it joy at all. I was burned out. My family and I were experiencing severe stress. I was having to cut back on my dental practice. My health was beginning to weaken—I was getting one cold after another, and my eyes were constantly bloodshot. Emotionally and spiritually, I felt as if I were suffering. But, as I looked back at what Jesus went through and at the martyrdom His disciples experienced, I wasn't suffering.

I wasn't suffering at all.

DONAHUE UPDATE: AUGUST 25, 1992

A remote broadcast from a brothel.

Gaining Strong Support

By this time, I had written Concerned Women for America several letters. Since they hadn't responded, I had given up hope that they would be interested in my campaign. However, on July 10 I received a phone call from Pattye Fava, the organization's national field director. They were considering authorizing me to use their name, but first she wanted to see some of the letters I had sent to advertisers and their responses. If you are asked for this kind of documentation, don't feel defensive. Organizations have to be sure they are dealing with trustworthy people, and not loose cannons.

I sent everything to her overnight and got a call back the next day. Even over the telephone I could sense her excitement. "This is really impressive!" she said. "I can't believe that you got these letters from such huge corporations and that they're pulling out of the *Donahue Show!*"

She went on to say, "We would like to do an article about your campaign in *Family Voice,* and we also want you to be a guest on *Beverly LaHaye Live,* a nationally syndicated program that goes out all over the country." That was the beginning of my relationship with Concerned Women for America, which has since become one of my staunchest supporters.

Getting into Focus

July 17 also brought me into contact with another powerful organization: Dr. James Dobson's Focus on the Family. Until that time, I hadn't received a response from any of the letters I had written to Dr. Dobson. I found out later that Focus receives hundreds of thousands of letters each month, and they have dozens of people employed simply to respond to the deluge. I had assumed Focus was merely Dr. Dobson and a couple of secretaries. How wrong I was!

I learned that one of their Community Impact seminars was coming to Dallas. These are outstanding seminars and particularly helpful if you're putting a campaign together.

The lecturer was Greg Jesson, a positive, upbeat man with his heart invested in his work. When I spoke with him, he told me, "This campaign of yours is exactly what our seminar is about—people like you getting involved in the community. And quite frankly, we don't have that many examples. If it's okay, I'd like to use your story as an example."

Not only did he use me as an example, but he allowed me to circulate my petition at the seminar. I was greatly encouraged by the support of Focus on the Family, and, as it turned out, I hadn't heard the last of them.

A Test of Faith

During this time, I saw several major sponsors drop *Donahue,* and yet others persistently refused.

I saw appalling, degrading broadcasts on the *Donahue* show, and yet I heard wonderful encouragement from people who believed in my efforts.

I had times of depression and self-doubt, and yet I experienced unparalleled spiritual growth.

The contrasts of light and dark, discouragement and hope, were astonishingly intense. Clearly, I was involved in more than a moral campaign. God was doing a deeper work within me.

DONAHUE UPDATE: SEPTEMBER 1, 1992

Male strippers and overweight strippers are featured.

I often thought that if my faith had been healthier, I wouldn't have found myself on such an emotional roller coaster ride. Instead, I would have been steadfast, confident that God was in total control. Some days I was able to say, "God is going to get the job done, and I don't have to worry about it." Other days, I was desperate for something great to happen, and when it didn't, I was discouraged.

I learned to treasure certain scriptures during those days, and a particularly significant one is Hebrews 10:38: "But my righteous one will live by faith. And if he shrinks back, I will not be pleased with him." Those are good words to remember when we feel that success is eluding us and we want to quit. Faith is what the Lord expects of us.

That's what He's planted in our hearts, and that's what He's nurturing and growing.

And as for success? Once we've done our best, success isn't our problem, it's His. He's quite capable of making the most of our feeble efforts. As Paul wrote, He is able "to do immeasurably more than all we ask or imagine, according to his power that is at work within us" (Ephesians 3:20).

CHAPTER SEVEN

Donahue Wasn't Laughing

July 21, 1992. *Receive a strongly worded, angry letter from the Donahue camp. I realize my efforts are beginning to hit the target, and I'm amazed.*

A number of times during the campaign I thought, "I would love to be a fly on the wall in the *Donahue* studios right now. I'd love just to be listening in." In actual fact, however, I didn't think the *Donahue* people were at all alarmed by what was going on with a dentist in Fort Worth. I assumed they were simply laughing at my campaign and blowing it off.

I was wrong.

On July 21 I found out that the *Phil Donahue* production people were well aware of the campaign. And they weren't laughing.

Everyday I went to the mailbox, looking forward to the letters I might receive. Picking up the mail felt a little like Christmas because over the months I received thousands of letters from all over the U.S. and Canada, and most of them were supportive and encouraging. There was very little hate mail.

That day, among the other correspondence, there was a letter from the president of Multimedia Entertainment in New York, a huge corporation which owns the rights to and distributes a large number of television programs, including *Donahue*. In fact, Phil Donahue himself is a major stockholder in Multimedia Entertainment.

The three-page letter was from Robert Turner, the president of Multimedia Entertainment, and as I began to read it, the anger and frustration of the writer virtually dripped off the page.

Excerpts from Turner's letter to Dr. Neill

Even though we can be totally assured that children are not viewing Donahue, I must emphasize the
pro-social nature of the Donahue show in contrast
to the distorted, incomplete and misleading
impression created by your partial list of topics
and limited excerpting of shows. Perhaps, Dr.
Neill you never viewed an entire show.

A "few minutes" of a Donahue show or a "nine
minute" tape condensation do not fairly present
the specific show's socially enlightening resolu-
tion or that show's place within the context of
all Donahue shows telecast in the previous and the
following weeks.

Donahue has always had the unique ability to cover
the entire spectrum of ideas, events, personali-
ties, lifestyles and the personal and public dra-
mas that make up the human scene worldwide. Within
this human spectrum, Dr. Neill, there will necessarily be issues that offend and distress some
individuals, but those same issues may inform,
entertain, or even educate someone else....

In conclusion, Dr. Neill, your letter attempts
economic blackmail with false and incomplete
information. You are harassing American advertisers who are fully and accurately informed of the
Donahue shows' content and their pro-social intent
as well as its adult target and viewing audience.
These advertisers choose Donahue on the recommen-
dation of media professionals whose express
responsibility it is to serve and protect the
advertiser.

Please review carefully these accurate facts and
figures about Donahue's topics and his audience.
Within this informed context, I am confident you
will realize that this "children's crusade" is
misguided and that your physical and mental ener-
gies on their behalf are being unfortunately mis-
directed.

I shot into the house yelling, "Christi, come here quick! Look at this! Look at this!" Until then, I had never imagined I would get the attention of the *Donahue* people. But now I definitely had their attention.

I lay in bed that night thinking, "Here's this multi-billion dollar company, and here I am with virtually no money by comparison, and I've made this giant—this Donahue empire—very, very angry." Then the spiritual warfare began in my mind. A thousand questions spun around, repeating themselves all night long: "What are they going to do to me? Are they going to threaten me? Am I going to start getting phone calls? Are they going to endanger my family? Are they going to attack my reputation? Are they going to sue me?"

Another recurring thought was, "I wonder if it's too late to back out of this campaign?"

Finally I got hold of my concerns and said, "Wait a minute. Is God in control of this or isn't He?" Several scriptures about fear became particularly meaningful and helpful to me at this time, including Exodus 14:13. When Moses was talking to Israelites, he said, "Do not be afraid. Stand firm and see the deliverance the LORD will bring you today. The Egyptians you see today you will never see again. The LORD will fight for you; you need only to be still."

That just blew my mind. There was Moses, leading the people out of their bondage to the powerful Egyptians, telling them, "Just sit tight. God's gonna take care of it." Even in the midst of my worst doubts, I could see He was doing exactly that for me as well.

And when the fear would return, and I would find myself worrying or feeling sorry for myself, I would read stories in the Bible about people whose faith wavered and yet God took care of them. I would hold on to great verses like Isaiah 41:10: "So do not fear, for I am with you; do not be dismayed, for I am your God. I will strengthen you and help you; I will uphold you with my righteous right hand."

When I read these verses, they gave me a magnificent sense of God's immense power. I can assure you, if you get into your own campaign, fear and discouragement will be at your heels from time to time, but God is greater, and just as He stood by me, He will stand by you.

The days following the receipt of Multimedia's letter were suspenseful because I didn't know what they were planning to do about me. And how should I respond to the letter? I finally decided the best response would be no response, fearing that whatever I said might be taken out of context and used against me.

So I didn't answer, and Robert Turner gave up on me. I never heard from him again. However, in the early months of the campaign, he apparently was Donahue's spokesman and was involved with all the media contacts. Later, Phil Donahue would speak for himself.

July 25, 1992. *Christi and I had a date tonight. It's so great just to be together. I thank the Lord for Christi.*

Earlier in the month we had dedicated ourselves to being more careful with our relationship. We both knew it was important to communicate often and to get away from the kids, the campaign, and the dental practice—to put everything aside. Those were wonderfully special times.

The book of Proverbs says, "He who has found a wife has found a good thing." I feel I have the most wonderful wife in the world. When we first married, I wasn't the strongest Christian. In fact, I was pretty weak. But Christi's steadfastness has had a great influence on me over our years together; she has really helped me grow in my faith.

During a campaign like ours, it's good to get out of town for a few days. Schedule times when you can go away for a weekend and completely separate yourself from the campaign for a while.

"That's It. I'm Quitting!"

July 28, 1992. *This morning I felt like giving up. All the major advertisers are ignoring me, and it seems this whole campaign is a waste of time. I'm considering quitting.*

When I got to work that morning, I called back to the house and said, "Christi, I don't want to do this anymore. I'm burned out. It's not working. The big national advertisers aren't pulling out, and I don't think they're going to." As I went on and on, she listened patiently on the other end of the line. Finally I said, "Christi, I want you to pray that God will get me out of this campaign gracefully. And if God wants me to do this, just pray that He'll show me."

I don't make it a habit to ask God for signs. In fact, I had never done it before, but in this case I needed some kind of supernatural encouragement. And if I didn't get it, I would assume He wanted me to drop the whole thing. After I hung up, I said, "Lord, You know my heart. You know I've done everything I can possibly do, and I don't seem to be getting anywhere. I'm quitting the campaign. If you don't want me to, let it be known. If not, it's over."

I was relieved. After work, I returned home in a great mood. I was laid back, and after I played with the kids, I went to bed without touching the campaign correspondence.

DONAHUE UPDATE: SEPTEMBER 18, 1992

Program subject: "Australian Male Strippers."

The next day, about one o'clock, my secretary slipped me a note: "Your wife's on the line."

I went to the phone.

Christi said, "You're not going to believe this!" She was screaming so loudly I had to pull the telephone away from my ear. I thought one of the kids was hurt.

"Settle down," I said. "What's going on?"

"You're not going to believe this, but we got a letter from the Dr Pepper Company...."

Dr Pepper was one of the top ten *Donahue* advertisers nationally.

"...we got a letter from the Dr Pepper Company, and they said they are withdrawing all their advertising from *Donahue* on a national basis."

There was a long silence.

"Are you still there?" Christi asked.

"Yeah. I'm here. Can you believe this?" Finally, we both praised the Lord over the telephone. Then, as I hung the phone up, I screamed out, "Yes!"

I caught myself right in the middle of the scream. It dawned on me that in a dental office screams are bad—very bad for business. If patients hear moans or screams, they assume we're torturing somebody in the next room.

A door behind my office opens into an alleyway. I went out that door and screamed so loudly the people in the apartment complex next door were probably ready to call 911. That was completely out of character, but that's how much the news about Dr Pepper meant to me.

I could then see what had happened. God had wanted my back to the wall. Otherwise, I might have taken the credit for it. Now it was clear He had done the work. God had once again proved Himself both wise and powerful.

When Dr Pepper pulled their commercials, they pulled them in every market across the country—over two hundred markets. That definitely had an impact on the *Donahue* people. There was no question about it: yes, I had their attention.

DONAHUE UPDATE: SEPTEMBER 29, 1992

Celebrating a lesbian wedding in Austin, Texas.

Making the Most of the Media

On July 30 another national radio network called and wanted to interview me on a news broadcast. In the wake of the big victory with Dr Pepper, I was feeling bold so I agreed to the interview, hoping the exposure would bring more pressure on the national advertisers who hadn't yet dropped *Donahue.* I sent out a letter to them by overnight delivery, letting them know I was going to be featured on a network radio interview in about a week's time.

When you're in the midst of a campaign, remember to use every possible opportunity with the media to help persuade the advertisers. Almost without fail when I reached an impasse with some of them, a news program or a reporter would contact me, wanting to do a story. These opportunities always gave me more leverage with the sponsors.

Let me reassure you that advertisers do not want controversy. The only reason they buy advertising time on a controversial show is because of the ratings. If they suspect a show is going to cause controversy, 95 percent of them will pull out. They want to advertise on top-rated programs, but they don't really want their names associated with controversial subject matter. So when you hold them accountable, and remind them that their names are going to be linked with something objectionable, they get nervous.

There are exceptions. Levi-Strauss, for example, revoked its funding to Boy Scouts of America because the organization refused to allow homosexual scout masters. A company with that philosophy wouldn't respond to a moral campaign like ours unless our efforts started hitting them emphatically in the pocketbook. However, most companies don't want to lose even one consumer, much less hundreds or thousands, so they make it their business to listen to consumers.

"Now We're Getting Somewhere!"

On August 2, Sara Lee Corporation, a huge television advertiser, withdrew their national advertisements from *Donahue*. Sara Lee has many subsidiaries under their corporate umbrella, and most of those companies were advertising on the *Donahue* program. The news that they were pulling out amounted to a huge victory.

On August 4, the *Donahue Show* was one of the most disgusting I had yet seen. Calling it his "Review of Nudity," Donahue featured male strippers, female strippers, homosexual strippers, and obese strippers. People appeared on stage completely nude, and they discussed masturbation and intercourse and showed pictures of a nudist colony.

Several sponsors withdrew after that broadcast.

The following day, as I was working on a patient, my secretary slipped me a note which said, "There's a gentleman from Kraft General Foods on the line."

When I answered the phone, he introduced himself and said, "We have a very large account with the *Donahue* program, as I'm sure you are aware. And we've decided that Kraft doesn't like its name being associated with programs like 'My Mother Is a Slut.' We've been monitoring the program and have decided that when our contract runs out in several weeks we will not renew it."

I was stunned. I wasn't sure I could trust my ears. Kraft was *Donahue's* biggest sponsor in 1992. "You're not going to renew?"

He repeated his statement. "That's correct. We're not going to renew our contract. We would appreciate it if you wouldn't let the media or the *Donahue* people know for a few weeks because we haven't told them yet."

After I finished with my patient, I made another quick trip out to the alley behind the office and screamed again.

DONAHUE UPDATE: OCTOBER 19, 1992

Program subject: "Interracial Relationships Among Homosexuals."

August 6, 1992. *I'm still on an emotional high. I had a hard time concentrating while I was praying this morning. I kept thinking, "God is so powerful!" I was praising Him, but I had a hard time praying about anything else.*

On August 13, Nestle, USA pulled out. Now Sara Lee, Kraft, and Dr Pepper had pulled out—all of them major national sponsors. Now an altogether new thought occurred to me: "We're actually getting somewhere! This campaign just might be successful after all."

DEALING WITH DISCOURAGEMENT

1. *Above all else, maintain a consistent prayer life. Be disciplined about praying and reading God's Word at a certain time every day.*

2. *Realize, from day one, that you are involved in heavy spiritual warfare and expect to be attacked.*

3. *Regularly read scripture that deals with spiritual warfare, discouragement, and the power of the Lord.*

4. *Pray the Psalms back to God. They are full of praise.*

5. *Find friends who are already involved in moral issues and become prayer partners with them. Make sure your prayer partners are optimistic individuals who are supportive of your campaign efforts.*

6. *Join a local chapter to the American Family Association, Concerned Women for America, or Christian Coalition and read their publications.*

7. *Stay focused on the finish line at all times—keep an eternal perspective. Remember that you are doing this for God's kingdom.*

8. *Get enough sleep.*

9. *Exercise regularly.*

10. *Whenever possible, get out of town for a few days. Don't take a cellular phone or a laptop computer. Leave the campaign behind.*

11. *If you have a family, set aside time consistently for "dates" with your spouse, and don't neglect your children. A campaign like this does not merit the sacrifice of your marriage and family.*

12. *Expect emotional highs and lows, and reflect upon the good times when the going gets tough.*

13. *Don't allow yourself to get disorganized. Sometimes discouragement*

can cause us to feel weary and therefore to fall behind on our work. Be disciplined, no matter how you feel.

14. *Anticipate apathy from others, and don't expect a lot of encouragement from other Christians, especially early on.*

15. *Don't give up!*

CHAPTER EIGHT

Donahue's Plans Backfire

August 24, 1994. *I've been asking God to open up another Christian media opportunity to let more people know about the campaign. There's nothing I can do about this, except wait on Him.*

C hristi was talking on the telephone when I got home from work. Just as I walked through the door, she looked up and said, "Oh, there he is!"

Excitedly, she put her hand over the receiver and whispered, "There's a man from Focus on the Family on the phone."

I went to my study where it would be quiet, away from all the kids. Focus on the Family might be a family-oriented ministry, but they didn't need to compete with my three children.

The man on the phone said, "This is Paul Hetrick, vice president of Focus on the Family." His voice had a note of concern. "There's a gentleman from New York City who has called Dr. Dobson several times in the last couple of days. Dr. Dobson didn't take the calls, but the man says he's representing the *Donahue Show.*"

Instantly I knew whom he was talking about, but all I said was, "Oh?"

"Yeah, this guy is trying to befriend us, but he doesn't have a whole lot of good to say about you. In fact he doesn't have anything good to say about you."

"Well, what's his name?" I asked—as if I didn't know.

"Robert Turner."

"From Multimedia Entertainment?"

"Yes."

My heart stopped. "Is he threatening a lawsuit?"

"No, he's not threatening a lawsuit. If they were going to sue you, they would have done it a long time ago since you've been working on this for several months." He asked, "Have you received any correspondence from Multimedia?"

"I've received one letter and I didn't respond to it."

"This man is trying to come across as a nice guy, and he's trying to persuade Dr. Dobson to use his influence to get you to back off."

Apart from my brief involvement with their Community Impact seminar, Focus on the Family knew nothing about me or my campaign. So Paul Hetrick asked me to express to them my research on the *Donahue Show*, everything I had sent to the advertisers, and their responses. I worked all the rest of the day, got everything together, and sent it overnight to Paul Hetrick.

During my prayer time the next morning, I asked the Lord to protect Focus on the Family from any spiritual warfare that might come their way because of my campaign. Later on that day, I gave an update to the USA Radio Network—my fifth interview with them. That afternoon Roman Meal Bread dropped their sponsorship, and Donahue aired a program from the Mustang Ranch Brothel.

August 27, 1992. *Paul Hetrick called back. It was like talking to a different man. I can't believe it—Focus on the Family wants to help me with the campaign!*

When Paul called again, I could hear the relief in his voice. After looking at the materials I'd sent him, he'd been pleased by my tactics and by the successes I'd had. He could see I wasn't placing undue pressure on Donahue's sponsors. He told me again, "Robert Turner is trying to convince Dr. Dobson to get you to back off. I'll send you a packet of things Turner has sent us."

In the packet were letters from fans to Donahue. Robert Turner wasn't well informed about what Dr. James Dobson stands for, as can be seen by the content of some of the letters, such as this one: "Being 23 and gay isn't easy, not at all, but I find it often easier now I can talk to my friends about it, and now that I have gay friends of my own. That might not have happened, had I not seen a certain *Donahue* episode when I was 14."

Then Paul said, "Dr. Dobson asked me to give a report on your campaign at our morning meeting. When I told them what you were doing, everybody cheered!"

I could hardly believe my ears. I'd been praying for a media contact, and God had opened the door to the biggest Christian media contact in the country.

Then Paul astonished me by inviting me to be a guest on a Focus on the Family radio broadcast on September 11. He said, "Dr. Dobson wants to give you the opportunity to tell your story to his listeners." Paul also asked if I would like to be featured in *Family News in Focus, Citizen* magazine, *Physician* magazine, and *Parental Guidance* magazine.

The irony of all this? Robert Turner had opened the doors for Dr. Dobson to generate new life in my campaign by trying to get him to squelch it.

I told Christi, "That's like the Mafia calling the FBI." The Lord couldn't have orchestrated it any better. After talking to Paul Hetrick, Christi and I prayed together, thanking the Lord for His provision, for opening doors with the media, and for causing some of Donahue's major sponsors to drop out. It seemed miraculous.

As I lay in bed that night, it occurred to me I had never dreamed I would be getting into all this. I had imagined writing twenty or thirty letters. At this point I had written over sixteen hundred letters to advertisers alone and probably another thousand to supporters.

DONAHUE UPDATE: OCTOBER 28, 1992

A stripper, a "fantasy sculptor," and an "erotic author" compare notes.

One Battle after Another

On September 2, one of *Donahue's* largest sponsors pulled out, but only on the condition of anonymity. This sponsor had been antagonistic toward me, causing some heated discussions on the telephone. One of their vice-presidents had said, "I think we have the right to sponsor any type of programming we want to."

"You're exactly right," I agreed. "You can sponsor anything you want. But let me ask you a personal question. You don't have to answer from a company standpoint, but just tell me personally. Would you want your children watching strippers and sadomasochists, a homosexual wedding ceremony, children discussing having sex at home, and a program originating from a brothel? Would you want that coming into your home?"

"No, I don't think I would," he said. "But at this company we believe in the first amendment right to free speech."

At that point, I got angry. "That's a cop-out, and you know it! I'm for free speech, too. But people like you hide behind the first amendment and use it as an excuse to sponsor filth and garbage!"

There was a brief pause. Then the man changed his tone. "Let me tell you something; you have a point. If you'll keep our name anonymous, we'll pull everything from *Donahue.*"

I was stunned. Right in the middle of the conversation he changed his mind.

When the campaign started, we had set a goal of four *Donahue* sponsors withdrawing by early fall. At this point—September 1992—sixty-seven sponsors had withdrawn, and many of their letters were a real encouragement to me.

The following are excerpts from some of the letters we received from the various sponsors:

Sponsor Excerpts

"The content of Mr. Donahue's recent programming has concerned us as well. Therefore we have instructed our media buying service to add the Donahue Show to our list of unacceptable programming. As such, Donahue will not be a part of any future buys. Thank you for sharing your concerns."
Baskin-Robbins USA., Co.

"Thank you for your letters of July 13th and July 26th regarding the Keebler commericals on the Donahue show. Upon receiving your first letter I notified our advertising agency that we wanted to cancel all of our commercial time on the Donahue show for the remainder of the year."
Keebler Company

"The purpose of this letter is to inform you that effective immediately we are stopping all advertising support (nationally and locally) of The Donahue Show for all Sara Lee Corporation divisions....Dr. Neill, we have a very strong desire to ensure that our brands are advertised on quality television programming and we share your concern for children's viewing. We thank you for your efforts to encourage better television."
Sara Lee Corporation

"Thank you for taking the time to write us and voice your concerns regarding our advertising on the Donahue Show. Let me assure you, Mr, Neill, it is Roman Meal Company's desire to avoid advertising in controversial and/or violent programs and that we pick programs that are family oriented. As a result of your letter and further review of the situation we have tightened our buying guidelines regarding program selection to specifically restrict from buying advertising during the Donahue Show as well as other controversial talk show programs."
Roman Meal Company

"I have just completed a careful study of your
comments about recent `Donahue' programming that
you found to be offensive. Your criticism certainly has merit based on the `Donahue' program
excerpts that you included with your letter.
Dillard Department Stores is committed to those
values that strengthen family unity; integrity,
value, common courtesty, and a respect for the
human character. With these values in mind we will
not advertise within any talk show that promotes
the material you outlined in your letter dated
June 6, 1992, including `Donahue.' We appreciate
your time and energy in making us aware of this
on-air program content."
Dillard Department Stores, Inc.

"Thank you very much for bringing to our attention
the programming content of the Donahue Show. We
wholeheartedly agree with your conclusion that it
has crossed the line into obscenity. Based on the
extreme programming content, and the fact that Lea
& Perrins only wants to be associated with fine,
upscale, family oriented programming, we have
decided to cancel all of our further advertising
on the Donahue show for the remainder of 1992 and
beyond. This will apply to every state in which
we advertise."
Lea & Perrins, Inc.

"While we cannot control the content of programming, we will not knowingly advertise on programs
which do not meet our policies. Obviously, the
Phil Donahue program is a problem, and I have
taken steps to remove any future advertising. We
will attempt to be more circumspect in the future.
It is through feedback from concerned individuals
such as yourself that we are able to correct our
actions when we stray."
Ross Laboratories

The Death of a Good Friend

September 3, 1992. *Sherry Reed died today.*

Our good friend Sherry had been diagnosed with cancer a couple years before. She had been doing well with her treatments, but the week before she had taken a turn for the worse. Suddenly, on September 3, she died.

Sherry's death reminded me of the brevity of our lives and that we need to make the best use of our time. Dr. Dobson often quotes Psalm 90:12: "Teach us to number our days aright, that we may gain a heart of wisdom."

I thought—again—that our children are not going to be in our homes forever. We're all just passing through. Our purpose on earth is to tell people about Christ and to make society better for future generations. That evening I made a new commitment to God to live my life for Him, and to make it count for eternity.

Another New Ally

When Paul Hetrick invited me to be a guest on Focus on the Family's radio show, he informed me that Don Wildmon would be sharing the broadcast with me. Don Wildmon is president of the American Family Association—a man I respect tremendously.

The American Family Association's primary focus is to combat excessive sex and violence on television. They have a monthly newsletter, which goes out to over a million people, that mentions the top sponsors and supporters of sleaze television.

Don has taken a tremendous amount of flak for his efforts over the past fifteen years. In his book *The Man the Networks Love to Hate,* he discusses just how much the television networks hate him. He also has ruffled feathers among church leaders because he's confronted their apathy and their unwillingness to get out into the world and take on sin and decadence. Only through the power and strength of the Lord has Don survived.

On September 10 Christi and I flew to Colorado Springs for the *Focus on the Family* broadcast. Needless to say, we were exhilarated about this new adventure. As I was buckling myself in, preparing for takeoff, I did a double take. Sitting across the aisle from me was Don Wildmon.

He was coming from Tupelo, Mississippi. I was coming from Fort Worth, Texas. Out of all the airlines that fly into Colorado Springs each day, several times a day, with hundreds of seats on each flight, Don Wildmon just happened to be sitting next to me.

After I introduced Christi and myself to Don, we discussed my campaign, and he asked if I had a list of advertisers that were being stubborn.

"Sure do," I smiled. "I was planning to give it you at the radio broadcast, but I'll give it to you now."

During the Dobson interview, Don Wildmon mentioned these companies by name.

DONAHUE UPDATE: NOVEMBER 12, 1992

Program subject: "Teenage Sex."

A Visit to Dr. Dobson's Headquarters

Naively I had envisioned Focus on the Family as residing in a small two-story building of three or four thousand square feet. I was wrong. As our guide explained, Focus has over a thousand employees and their ministry headquarters is housed in a huge office building that is several stories high. I was struck by the enormity of it all.

September 11, the day of the taping, was a wonderful occasion for us to meet a number of the people who make Dr. Dobson's ministry so successful, including Dr. Dobson himself. As we did the taping that afternoon, I was impressed by the way he makes his guests feel relaxed and calm. He's very down to earth. I remember sitting there with Mike Trout and Dr. Dobson, thinking, "I can't believe I'm in the same room with these guys. They have been fighting this battle for years."

Don Wildmon made a comment during the interview that has stuck with me: "If we had ten other people in big markets around the country doing what Richard is doing, Donahue would be gone." At first I thought he was overstating the facts, but when I thought about it, I knew he was right. If one person in New York, one in Los Angeles, one in Miami, and a few others in the bigger cities around the country waged a campaign similar to mine, Phil Donahue would not be on the air any longer.

If men and women—people like you—each focused his or her attention on one objectionable television show, the airwaves would be cleaned up.

My primary motivation for writing this book? To encourage you to join the battle!

DONAHUE UPDATE: NOVEMBER 17, 1993

Women who hate sex explain why.

CHAPTER NINE

The Spy Who Wanted to Be Seen

September 14, 1992. *The good news is that 75 percent of the front-line Donahue sponsors in Dallas/Fort Worth are gone. The bad news is that other advertisers are quickly taking their place.*

After the emotional high of the Dobson taping, I experienced a tremendous letdown when I returned home. As I took a close look at the advertisers, I realized we were dealing with a "second wave" of national sponsors. A highly-rated show like Phil Donahue's has reserve sponsors, which it quickly plugs into the gaps when necessary.

If you're launching a campaign like mine, remember that a large number of advertisers have to withdraw before a station will take the show off the air, and the higher the show's audience ratings, the more sponsors have to drop out. In Lynda Beam's campaign, 107 advertisers withdrew from the *Geraldo Show.* Geraldo didn't have extremely high ratings, so after losing that many, the station didn't have enough sponsors left to keep it on the air.

In mid-September 1992, my guess was that it would take more than 107 dropped sponsors to get Donahue off the air. I did notice one good thing, however. Many of the reserve sponsors were family-oriented companies. Nonetheless, for the time being, it seemed I was never going to get the job done.

On September 14, Revlon and Ocean Spray, both second-wave sponsors, dropped Donahue. It was always encouraging to see a major corporation drop out, even though they sometimes said, "We were doing research on our advertising, and we happen to have come to the conclusion—just by coincidence—that *Donahue* isn't a program we want to advertise on."

Don't be discouraged by that sort of evasion. The point is, the sponsor has dropped out. Whether the sponsors want to admit it was because of your campaign or not, they have pulled their advertising dollars out of the program. That's fine with me; I don't care if I get the credit. What's important is that they've taken a stand, and I appreciate them for doing that.

Trusting God through the Low Times

Having always been a stable person, I've never had a problem with ups and downs—at least not until I started my campaign. This has been a new experience for me, in an emotional sense. And I learned that even when there were lulls in the action God was working behind the scenes, according to His plan. He was working on the hearts of the advertisers. He was working on the media. He was working on Donahue's people, as evidenced by Robert Turner's call to James Dobson.

So don't get discouraged, even if there's a lull. Things are happening as long as you're being obedient. The danger lies in our human tendency to get antsy and to want to make faster progress. Even though I know better, I find myself slipping into that stance from time to time.

By now, I had written 2,342 letters to sponsors, and eighty had pulled out. On September 22, General Mills, another huge advertiser on *Donahue,* dropped him in every market across the country. At the same time, Christi and I began to notice an increase in public service announcements during *Donahue* broadcasts, which further indicated a loss of advertising revenues.

Although things were moving along quite well, I had a secret fear I might still be running this campaign ten years hence—an idea that didn't exactly excite me. It seemed like a good time for something encouraging to happen, but that's not what I got.

A New Kind of Trouble

On September 25, I was working on a patient when Alice Schroeder, my dental hygienist, called me aside and quietly inquired, "Is your insurance agency checking out your car for some reason?"

I stared at her blankly and shook my head. "No. Why?"

"Well," she shrugged, "there was a guy outside taking pictures of your car. He was using a camera with a huge flash, and it was bright out there, so I don't know why he needed a flash at all. Anyway, after he finished, he got into a late model, dark blue sedan and took off."

I shook my head. "That's weird...."

"Yeah," Alice agreed. "It was like he wanted to draw attention to himself."

I didn't give it a second thought.

DONAHUE UPDATE: NOVEMBER 18, 1992

Homosexuals give details about their lifestyles and love life.

Later that day I sent Becky Creed, one of my secretaries, to the post office. As she went up to the counter to buy stamps, she was vaguely aware of a man behind her. He approached her and remarked, "Dr. Neill sure is mailing a lot of letters these days, isn't he?"

She laughed and responded, "Oh, yeah, he's working on this Donahue campaign."

The man stared at her sternly for a moment, then turned around and stalked out of the post office.

Becky shivered and asked herself, "How in the world does he know who I am?" Unnerved, she stayed inside the post office for nearly thirty minutes, not wanting to run into him outside. She knew about the man Alice had seen, and assumed she was dealing with the same person.

When she finally went out to her car, the man was sitting behind the wheel of a dark blue sedan parked nearby, obviously the one Alice had described. He just sat there, staring at Becky, and when she left, so did he.

Becky rushed back to the office and told Alice and me what had happened. After comparing notes, they agreed. "It's the same guy following us around."

Several similar incidents happened over the next couple of days. I tried to figure out who might be responsible for such harassment. WFAA, the local ABC affiliate? The *Donahue Show?* Multimedia in New York? The advertisers? There really wasn't anybody else.

A few days before, a relative of mine from Chicago had asked, "What if Phil Donahue is involved with the Mafia?" At the time, I had laughed it off. Now it wasn't so funny.

I thought about my wife. My kids. My employees. My friends. And I started calling around to get advice. El Arnold, at the Dallas Association for Decency, advised me to call the police right away. So I called Jeff Dunn, a friend of mine at the Fort Worth Police Department. He wasn't in, but his wife promised he would call me as soon as possible.

DONAHUE UPDATE: NOVEMBER 23, 1992

Transsexuals analyze how a male becomes a female.

John Clemens, at USA Radio Network, advised me, "The best thing you could do right now is to bring it out in the open and get the media involved. The more the media is involved, the less likely it is that anyone would harm you." That didn't exactly give me a great feeling. In fact, I was more nervous than ever. I kept thinking, "Why did I ever get involved in this campaign in the first place? I don't want anyone to get hurt!"

That, of course, is precisely what the man in the blue car wanted me to think.

Finally, Allen Wildmon, Don's brother who is with the American Family Association, laid my deepest fears to rest. "The worst thing they could possibly do to you right now is to harm you or your family," he explained. "They know it would be a public relations' nightmare if they did anything to you. They're not about to hurt you. Besides, when you think about it, if they seriously wanted to hurt you, you'd never see them. That guy wanted to be seen because he's trying to intimidate you. Don't you let it bother you. It happens all the time. Just blow it off."

I felt Allen's words were God's way of reassuring me, so I began to relax. Then Jeff Dunn, the policeman, called me back. He laughed, "What you ought to do when you see that fellow is walk right up to him and say, 'Hey, how are you doing? I'm Richard Neill, and I've noticed you're pretty interested in me. Do you want to have a cup of coffee?'"

We never saw the man in the blue car again, so I never got the chance.

Back on the Roller Coaster

After the *Focus on the Family* broadcast aired on September 25, I got an unbelievable number of phone calls from supporters all over the country. Letters poured in for months. *Focus on the Family* airs on over two thousand stations across the nation, and the positive response I received through his interview was incredible.

But then the roller coaster began its descent again. On September 29, two of my employees were sick, and we were an hour and a half behind schedule all day long. I also got five blow-off letters from companies, the most I had ever received in one day. And WFAA had brought in a new stable of sponsors to fill in the open spots on *Donahue.*

Those days come and go during a campaign, and at the time I was "weary in welldoing." Fortunately, God had a plan to lift my spirits again.

October 1, 1992. *Don Wildmon called. He's willing to help me out, and I really appreciate his concern. He knows what this battle is all about, and I respect his efforts on the front lines of the battle for decency in our country.*

I hadn't talked to Don Wildmon since our meeting in Colorado Springs. He asked me to send him a list of twenty *Donahue* advertisers, which sounded like great news to me, because the American Family Association has over a million people in the organization, many of whom are genuine activists in cleaning up television.

I was relieved that he was willing to help, but I had no idea to what extent he was intending to go. Don Wildmon made my campaign the AFA monthly project for November. He sent out postcards for people to mail in to the twenty sponsors, and the advertisers received thousands and thousands of them. Then they began to drop like flies.

At a time when I needed it most, Don was a lifesaver.

October 6, 1992. *Eighty-seven sponsors have withdrawn, including Arby's, Worthington Foods, and HUD. Thank you, Jack Kemp!*

Even though I knew HUD was a major *Donahue* sponsor, I thought it would be a waste of time to write to them since they are a governmental agency. Then one day I remembered something important—the man responsible for HUD just might agree with the values behind my campaign. Jack Kemp, who is a staunch conservative, is the secretary of Housing and Urban Development. So I wrote a letter to him.

Later on, I learned that the minute Kemp realized what kind of programming was on *Donahue,* he said, "Let's get off." That was the end of HUD as a *Donahue* sponsor. And it would have happened sooner, if I had thought to write.

Time for Family R & R

By mid-October, Lynda Beams was encouraging me to have a press conference, and I was trying to assure her it wasn't a good idea. During her campaign, she had found that a press conference applied pressure on the local CBS affiliate. She held her press conference at a hotel in Dallas, invited all the media to come, and had a good turnout.

Not long afterward, the CBS affiliate dropped *Geraldo*.

She had her press conference when only twenty-four advertisers had withdrawn. By now I had seen eighty-seven withdraw, and the secular media still didn't know what was happening.

WFAA wasn't telling anybody.

Donahue and Multimedia weren't telling anybody.

If anyone was going to break the story to the secular media, it would have to be me. And I wasn't ready.

DONAHUE UPDATE: DECEMBER 17, 1992

Program Subjects: Masturbation and condoms.

As always, I dreaded the brutality of the secular media. Furthermore, I was having eye problems. My vision was fine, but my eyes were chronically bloodshot due to lack of sleep and being physically run-down.

Fortunately, the time had rolled around for our annual family vacation. That particular year, we had decided to take the kids to Orlando, Florida, for ten days. At first, I'd been tempted to take my computer along and write letters while we were gone, but one look in the mirror was enough to convince me otherwise. And Christi had a few suggestions along similar lines. For the first time in the campaign, I decided not to take anything Donahue-related.

I needed rest, fun, and diversion. My family needed my undivided attention. I left the whole campaign behind me in Fort Worth, packed up, and left town without looking back. God was quite capable of taking care of everything in my absence, and I decided to let Him do so.

It was the best decision I had made in a very long time.

CHAPTER TEN

Nothing More to Lose

O ver the Christmas holidays the number of Donahue's advertisers appeared to have diminished dramatically. We determined this by keeping track of the number of public service announcements that aired during his broadcasts. Whenever several sponsors withdrew, the number of PSAs increased. At last count there had been eighteen PSAs in one broadcast. Things seemed to be going well.

Then, on December 28, 1992, I hit a brick wall. As I sat reviewing the *Donahue Show* that day, I was stunned. One new advertiser followed another. From an average of sixteen PSAs per day, the number abruptly dropped to three. And the advertisers were tough—Time Warner, the *National Enquirer, Star Magazine*—companies that didn't seem particularly interested in family or morality.

Sitting there, dejected and discouraged, I wondered if they would just continue to add new sponsors indefinitely. Robert Turner, president of Multimedia Entertainment, had once claimed there were over three thousand sponsors available. "If that's the case," I told myself, "I figure it will take about twenty-three years to get Donahue off the air in Dallas."

I was worn down.

The hard truth was, I really wanted to get out of the whole thing.

Some Unwanted Interest

December 30, 1992. *The* National Enquirer *called. The last place I want to see myself is on the cover of a tabloid at the market checkout line. I didn't return their call, and don't intend to.*

I was doing a root canal on a patient when one of my secretaries walked in and handed me a little yellow Post-It that said, "Well, I guess your campaign has hit the big time—or is it the slime time? The *National Enquirer* is on the line."

"Oh, no!" I said emphatically.

Big professional mistake. That's not appropriate behavior for a dentist when he's working on a patient. For all the patient knew, I was panicked about her tooth, or had dropped a root canal file down her throat, or had slipped with the drill and made a huge hole in the wrong place. Her eyes got as big as saucers.

I quickly explained that I'd received a call from the *National Enquirer* and told Cheryl to inform them I wouldn't take the call.

But they didn't give up. In fact, after that, several other tabloid papers started calling. *The Star. The Sun.* It was odd, because all those reporters had British accents. They called the office and the house, but I never talked to any of them.

If you are involved in a campaign, you too will probably receive calls from the tabloids. I would strongly recommend not doing interviews with the *National Enquirer, The Star,* or any of the other sensational papers. I made a similar decision about appearing on exploitative television. These media "opportunities" may bring attention to a campaign, but in many ways they cheapen our efforts and involve us in the very things we are fighting against.

Back to the Basics

January 2, 1993. *Greg took his first steps today—what a celebration!*

During this time of disappointment, I found myself more drawn toward my family—the people I love most. An unusual sentimentality had taken root in my heart, and I was more keenly aware of their importance to me than I'd ever been before. The new year began, and as far as I was concerned, the most significant aspect of its arrival was that our Greg, a December baby, was now a year old.

"People Who Love Sex Addicts."

On January 2, I was sitting at my desk in the study watching the snow fall and the girls outside, slipping and sliding around and having a great time. As I marveled at the beauty of the snow, I realized I had missed a lot of God's beauty since the campaign began. It had been snowing for three days, and I'd hardly noticed it. Impulsively, I shoved my work aside and went out to have a snowball fight with the children.

Whenever I'd let go of the campaign for even a few moments, I always had a nagging sense that I was not staying on top of things. Yet, as I look back, I can unquestionably see that God was working powerfully behind the scenes, no matter what I was doing. When you're in the middle of a storm, you can't see anything—not even your hand in front of your face. But, when the storm is over, everything becomes clear and well defined. Early January was a dead period in the campaign, but God was at work.

Later on that same snowy day, all five of us were in the breakfast room. For three weeks Greg had been trying to pull up and stand by himself. He'd wobble around for a few seconds and then plop back down. Christi held his hand, and he took a couple of steps. But this time when she let go, he continued to stand. He was stunned.

The girls started chanting, "Go, Greg, go. Go, Greg, go. Go, go, go, go!" It was like a pep rally.

He took a step, and his eyes got real big. The girls started screaming and cheering. He took another step, and fell. We got him up again, and he took one step, and then another. At that point everybody lost control. The girls started cheering again and running through the house and shouting.

In the midst of our excitement, that recurring thought struck me again—"Enjoy the children while they're little. They aren't going to be with you that long."

Like a new companion, a sense of time's rapid passing and the importance of making the most of our days on earth accompanied me throughout the campaign. Sometimes it speeded me up in my efforts, and at other times it slowed me down, reminding me to "stop and smell the roses."

Recognition: Pro and Con

A few days later one of my assistants asked, "Have you ever heard of Howard Stern?"

I said, "Unfortunately, I have." The best thing I can say about him is that he makes Phil Donahue look like a saint.

She continued, "My husband was listening to Howard Stern this morning, and Geraldo Rivera was his guest."

I looked at her blankly. "Oh, okay."

"They were talking about you."

I laughed. "I bet that was a real positive discussion."

"Howard Stern asked Geraldo, 'What do you think about this dentist in Fort Worth who's trying to get Donahue off the air?' Geraldo talked about it a little bit, then Stern said, 'Well, I think they ought to go after you guys. They're trying to get me off the air, and you're just as bad.'"

He wasn't far from the truth.

Fortunately for me, that was the extent of the discussion, but it struck me as quite interesting. My campaign had barely been reported in Fort Worth, yet in New York it had traveled through the media grapevine and apparently was a familiar topic among the talk show hosts.

About this same time I received a letter from a man whom I have highly regarded for a long time—Charles Colson. Colson's testimony and ministry have always touched and inspired me. Early in the campaign, in response to a letter I wrote him, he had jotted a handwritten message, "Keep up the good work." I continue to treasure both letters, and again I realized that people were aware of my efforts, and at least a few were applauding.

And what was Donahue doing? Featuring "Great Sex Every Time," a discussion of orgasms. Without question, it was adult programming, something that shouldn't be on network television, day or night.

Preparing for the Press Conference

By February, Lynda Beams and I concluded the time had come for the long-awaited press conference.

First of all, let me explain why a press conference is important. In a campaign or any newsworthy effort, the media will be your friend or your enemy. Either way, you are at their mercy unless you make the facts available to them—the facts as you want them understood.

The most efficient way to do this is to invite all the media in your area to one public location at a specific time. In addition to speaking to them, you can provide them with written information, and you can answer their questions. If the event is well attended, you may see yourself on the evening news and read about yourself in the newspaper. These are intimidating possibilities to nearly anyone, so it is important to be extremely well prepared for a presentation to the press.

Having said that, I would be less than honest if I didn't tell you that my press conference was a disaster, or at least it felt that way at the time. We rented a room at the Loew's Anatole, a posh hotel in Dallas, and sent out a press release notifying all the media. And we invited everybody—the *New York Times*, the Associated Press, the *Dallas Morning News*, the *Fort Worth Star-Telegram*, and all the local television and radio stations. I practiced my presentation again and again.

The trouble started the day before the press conference when I began to get laryngitis. I went home early and tried not to talk. I would need every bit of my vocal strength the next day—or so I thought.

The Press Conference

The press conference is a valuable tool for several reasons.

- It draws media attention to your cause.
- It informs the media about your campaign successes—the number of sponsors that have dropped the show in question, and the sponsors that have not yet withdrawn their advertising dollars. I recommend waiting until over fifteen or twenty advertisers have pulled out—a newsworthy number—before breaking the story at a press conference.
- It puts pressure on the local television affiliate. This is especially true when you contact the FCC in conjunction with the press conference at which you expose explicit programming.
- It enables you to read and give out a concisely written press release, stating all the valuable information that is necessary and relevant to your campaign.
- It provides a controlled setting in which you can answer questions about your campaign.

Here are the steps you'll need to take to organize your press conference:

1. Determine where the press conference will be held. It's important that the location be easily accessible to the mass media.

2. Decide whom you will invite, but include representatives of both the Christian and the secular media. Involve reporters from local radio and television stations, newspapers, the Associated Press, and any national media that might find the story interesting. Once you have compiled a list, call each office to find out the fax number of the news room and the name of the appropriate contact person in the news room.

3. Type out an announcement to fax to the contact person in each media news department. Send the fax four to five days before the press conference. Then resend the fax one day prior to the press conference. By sending the fax message twice, you can be sure it is received and distributed properly.

This announcement is a teaser, to stimulate interest. It provides the time, location, and other basic details of the press conference. Also, in a couple of sentences, it should capsulize what the press conference will be about without telling the whole story. If you provide too much information, the reporter may not show up but instead just write his story from the fax message.

4. Type out your press release, double spaced, on legal size paper. Provide the date, your name (or the contact person you've designated), your complete address, and your phone number, (or the phone number of the contact person that you've designated).

Mine was three pages long and included much the same information as my first letter to the sponsors. My press release...
   • explained how I got started;
   • introduced the issue of sleaze programming;
   • named the groups that supported me;
   • provided a listing of topics and quotes from past Donahue shows;
   • and stated precisely what I was asking WFAA to do.

5. Hold a mock press conference with a group of your supporters and practice your delivery. Brainstorm with questions and answers.

The Big Event

February 10, 1993. *The press conference, and the most humiliating day of the campaign. Never again!*

I started out the day irritable and nervous. I was so short with Christi I had to ask her forgiveness later on. I don't remember ever feeling quite that uptight in my life. We arrived an hour early at the hotel, where we met Bob and Lynda. The room was set up, and we acted out one last practice session of questions and answers, as I continually looked at my watch.

About thirty minutes before the press conference, my brother John showed up. The press would be arriving soon so they could set up their TV cameras. Lynda was especially optimistic because she had attracted a good representation of media at her press conference.

Twenty minutes until press conference time. Nobody had showed up.

Fifteen minutes. Nobody was there.

Ten minutes. Still nobody.

Five minutes before the press conference was to start Steven Cole Smith from the *Fort Worth Star-Telegram* arrived. I had spoken to him several times before, and he had already reported on my campaign—and in a fair and respectful manner. He said, "A lot of times people show up late. Don't worry about it."

But no one ever showed up, except Steve Smith.

You can imagine my thoughts. "This is a disaster. Nobody cares about this campaign. No television stations, no radio stations, no print media—nobody." I felt like crawling in a hole, disappearing, and forgetting the whole thing.

Steve Smith saw me totally humiliated. He saw me in an entirely different light than he might have if I had been up at the podium, reading my press release to fifty people. Perhaps he felt sorry for me, because before he left, he gave me the names and numbers of some of the more conservative radio talk show hosts in the Dallas/Fort Worth area. "You really ought to call these guys. They'll help you out," he said as he left.

"You just call me if anything comes up, or there's anything I can do."

As it turned out, Steve Smith would be the reporter to cover Phil Donahue's visit to Fort Worth several months later. I am convinced that my "failed" press conference caused him to treat me with more kindness and respect, and to positively influence other reporters as well.

After he left, Bob and Lynda came in, and we talked for a couple of minutes. They didn't look particularly distressed, but I'm sure they were keeping their spirits up for my sake. Ultimately, Christi and I were left sitting in that hotel room by ourselves, doing some deep soul searching. In an hour and a half, we said very little.

"Christi," I told her, "that's it. God knows I've done everything I can possibly do. I've spent a lot of money on this campaign. I've promoted it as best I can. I've had this press conference. I've done everything I could think of. What a total disaster."

When we got home, there was a message on the answering machine from a local Christian newspaper, wanting a story on my press conference.

I returned the call, saying, "I'd love to talk to you, but to be honest I don't think I'm going to be involved in this anymore. I'm quitting. As a matter of fact, I've got laryngitis, so I don't even want to give you an interview at all. Sorry."

The next morning I woke up feeling reprieved. I like to succeed at whatever I do, and I never want to leave a job undone, but this campaign obviously was not going to succeed. It was time to get on with my life and to allow our home to return to normal. Christi was relieved. I was relieved.

The campaign was over, and that was just fine with me.

DONAHUE UPDATE: MARCH 12, 1993

Program subject: Homosexual priests.

Nothing to Lose

The next day, February 12, I awakened with a strange idea running through my mind—I would call the *New York Times*. It was particularly peculiar because I had decided the campaign was finished, and because I've never been one to seek publicity. So why did I call? Just for a kick, I suppose.

When I phoned them, I learned the name of their primary entertainment writer—Bill Carter. I thought, "Even though the campaign is over, why not stir things up? I've got nothing to lose."

So I did.

I not only talked to Bill Carter once, but he called back several times to get more information on the story. He, in turn, called Phil Donahue. He called the sponsors. He called Robert Turner. And I just sat back and waited. My perspective was, "Whatever happens, happens." I didn't care that much about what he wrote because none of my friends read the *New York Times* anyway.

As it turned out, I should have been a little more nervous.

DONAHUE UPDATE: MARCH 25, 1993

Program subject: "Priests Who Have Sex with Young Boys."

THE DAY OF THE PRESS CONFERENCE

1. *Review your questions and answers.*

2. *Show up at your site one hour early, making sure the room is ready and everything is in order.*

3. *Have twenty-five to thirty copies of the press release available for distribution.*

4. *When the media arrives, begin no later than ten minutes after the stated press conference time.*

5. *Pass out your press release no more than thirty seconds before you go to the podium. If you pass it out fifteen or twenty minutes early, the media representatives will have a chance to read through it, and you may be hit with tougher questions.*

CHAPTER ELEVEN

Donahue's Coming to Town

February 18, 1993. *By the time the* New York Times *article appeared, I had forgotten all about it. Fortunately, it did exactly what I wanted it to do—it stirred things up.*

I started seeing patients at eight that morning. At half past eight, my secretary slipped me a note: "Two radio stations, one in Los Angeles and one in Washington, D. C., are on the line. They want interviews."

"Interviews?" My mind was blank. "Why in the world would they be calling today?" Then it came back to me that today was the eighteenth, the day the *New York Times* article was to appear. "I'd better read the article before I talk to anybody."

I immediately sent one of my assistants to purchase a paper. As I rustled through the pages, I found it—on the front page of the business section. To my surprise, it was both lengthy and prominently displayed.

Of course, there was no pro-Richard Neill spin; in fact I wouldn't say it was a fair depiction of the campaign. For one thing, Bill Carter reported that originally I had called the *New York Times* looking for media attention. He presented me as a publicity seeker, not as a concerned parent, and he also stated that some of the sponsors who had dropped *Donahue* denied that I had anything to do with their decision.

Overall, however, I had expected their coverage to be much worse than it was. And it served the purpose I wanted it to serve, which was to catalyze the situation. As my parting shot, I wanted to give Phil Donahue something to think about.

Anyway, my campaign was over. What did I care?

By half past nine that morning, two more radio stations had called, one from Miami, another from New York City. By the end of the day, nine more had called. This pattern continued for two weeks, during which more than sixty radio shows contacted me, and I talked with them all.

DONAHUE UPDATE: MAY 13, 1993

Program subject: "Lesbian Love Match."

If you had asked me a year before if I would have made myself available for all those interviews, I would have said, "Absolutely not. I won't talk to any of them." However, in the meantime, the Lord had put me in touch with people who had prepared me for dealing with the media. He had also brought me to the end of myself, and therefore my personal insecurity, through the press conference debacle. My preparation was complete, and I was quite willing to talk to every interviewer who called. In fact, it got to be fun.

SAMPLE QUESTIONS AND ANSWERS

Q. *Do you consider yourself part of the religious right? Are you a fanatic?*

A. Those are your words, not mine. This campaign spans all types of religious belief or non-belief. I have friends and patients who are Catholic, Protestant, Moslem, conservative, and liberal. All of them think sleaze programming has gone too far. Since the beginning of time, it's been the number one priority of every civilization to protect their children. And I don't see why our civilization should be any different.

Q. *This type of programming must be what the public wants. Do you think these shows would exist if there weren't a market for them?*

A. That's an interesting question. Donahue stated that he would love to have an execution on his program. He would love to see the bad guys fry. Often what draws people in is the shock value of it all. The producers shock people with broadcasts about sadomasochism, transsexuals, and people talking about encouraging their kids to have sex at home. Robert Turner, the president of Multimedia Entertainment, has admitted that the stripper programs were just ratings grabbers.

Q. *Shouldn't it be the parents' responsibility to monitor what children watch?*

A. Yes and no. I believe that the responsibility for protecting children from sleaze programming lies squarely on the shoulders of the producers of the programs.

Let me explain. Many times both parents, concerned parents, have to work to make ends meet. Or, in a single parent family, the parent has to work one or two jobs just to provide for the family. In situations like this, children may stay home sick, or come home from school with no parental supervision at all. During summer, they are home all day. They flip on the television, and they watch trash television because it fascinates them.

In any civilized society with rights, there must be equivalent responsibilities. The producers must be responsible.

Q. *Are you threatening the sponsors?*

A. No, I'm trying to help the sponsors. I'm being an information source to them. Many CEOs of large corporations don't have time to monitor the programs on which they are advertising. They simply buy their advertising by ratings numbers.

I'm alerting the CEOs of these companies to the nature of the programming they're supporting, and asking them if this is really what they want their company associated with. Ninety-eight percent of the sponsors are very receptive to withdrawing from indecent programming; only 2 percent are not.

When dealing with the unresponsive 2 percent, it's the responsibility of the consumer to stand up and make his voice heard. We need to hold the sponsors accountable for the kind of programming that they're supporting. They, in turn, need to hold Phil Donahue accountable.

Q. *What do you say to Phil Donahue's claim that you are taking excerpts of his program out of context?*

A. That's an interesting claim, because Donahue features some of the most deviant forms of sexual activity imaginable. Many times the whole program is centered totally around this deviant behavior.

Over two hundred corporate advertisers pulled their advertising, and many of these advertisers wrote to me, "Thank you for the information you've sent us, but in all fairness to the *Donahue Show* we need to do some research. We need to order some tapes and transcripts and research this ourselves. We'll get back with you in two months and let you know our decision."

Invariably they called or wrote later on and said, "You're absolutely right. We've watched the whole program, and we want nothing to do with this type of programming."

Q. *Are you a Christian?*

A. Absolutely. I can't deny my faith, and I would never want to. But my Christianity is not the issue. The issue is, "Should children be exposed to topics such as sadomasochism, transsexuals, and other deviant forms of behavior?" Phil Donahue wants to avoid the issue. That's why he wants to talk about my faith and the faith of the people who are unhappy with his program. He has no other defense.

Q. *Don't you believe in the first amendment right to free speech?*

A. Yes. In a civilized society, you must have both rights and responsibilities. Recently in Dallas, there was a toxic waste spill near a day care center. The parents of the children in that day care were up in arms. The public was enraged. Everyone held the company accountable and demanded they deal with the pollution that was being spilled into the environment. The company was responsible and cleaned up the pollution. Television is no different. The producers of these types of programs must be responsible and clean up the pollution coming out over the airwaves.

February 19, 1993. *I'm not sure how much good all this radio coverage is doing. It's nice for the ego, but I don't think it's really accomplishing anything. I still plan to quit.*

On February 19, four Canadian stations called. On February 22, I had interviews with eleven programs in one day—including New York, Los Angeles, Seattle, West Palm Beach, and St. Louis.

On February 23, Daryl Gates, the former police chief in Los Angeles, interviewed me on his radio show. Gates is quite conservative and therefore very much on my side. I had become accustomed to dealing with antagonistic radio interviewers, and despite his controversial reputation Gates's positive attitude was a shot in the arm.

That night I was interviewed by Gil Gross on the CBS radio network. During our ten minute conversation, Gross asked me to name some of the things I didn't like about the *Donahue* program. I mentioned issues like having programs about strippers, transsexuals, and a cafeteria worker who described having sex with a young boy.

He started laughing, trying to make light of my campaign.

I said, "Wait a minute, I'm not through." Then I caught him off guard by repeating some of the sleaziest quotes I had from the program.

"Whoa! Whoa! Wait a minute. Okay. That's enough," he interrupted, alarmed that I was talking about such things on the air.

"That's exactly my point. You have a problem with quotes and excerpts from the *Phil Donahue Show,* and yet you stand behind the first amendment and say that children should be exposed to that kind of stuff on daytime programming."

He was on my side for the rest of the interview. He said, "You know, I think you're right. This stuff really is bad."

I couldn't have known that God was using those interviews to prepare me for the *real* media onslaught just ahead. I'll repeat what I've said before—God is always doing something behind the scenes, and He brings forth His best work when you least expect it.

Big Offer from New York

March 10, 1993. *God knows I've done everything I can do. I'm emotionally and spiritually spent. I have no desire to keep going because I've exhausted every media avenue I have.*

I wrote those words in my diary early in the morning on March 10. Later that day, once again I was working on a patient as Rhonda, my secretary, slipped me a note. This one said, "I think you'd better step out into the hall."

Anxiety gripped me as I excused myself from my patient.

"There's this lady on the phone," Rhonda explained, "and I think you'd better speak to her."

"Who is she?"

"Her name is Patricia McMillan." Rhonda was looking at me rather strangely.

"Well, who is that? I've never heard of her."

"Patricia McMillan is the producer of the *Donahue Show.*"

My jaw dropped. "Yes!" I shouted.

I had never quite believed that Donahue would be alarmed enough to confront me personally. Now it was as if someone had taken a big hypodermic needle full of raw energy and injected it into my arm. From that point on, I was back in the campaign.

DONAHUE UPDATE: MAY 18, 1993

Teenage strippers explore their way of life.

Meanwhile, Patricia McMillan was still on hold. When I picked up the receiver, she introduced herself and said, "I'm the producer of the *Donahue Show.* And we're very interested in what you're doing down there in Fort Worth."

I thought to myself, "I bet you are."

"Phil's interested too," she continued. "He's a very nice person, and he wants to be very fair about it all. So he's decided to invite you to be on his program."

"Well, thank you," I responded. "That's very thoughtful of you to invite me to do that."

Her voice was pleasant and kind. "We're sensitive to the fact that you have a dental practice and that you can't get away from the office for very long. So we've decided to bring the program to you. We're going to rent the Tarrant County Convention Center, which holds almost three thousand people, and we want you to be a part of the program. You can come on by yourself, or you can bring several people with you if you want."

Besides inviting me to appear on the show, she also offered to give me half the tickets for my constituents. I had decided several months before, when I'd talked to Dr. Dobson and Don Wildmon, that I was never going to accept an invitation to be on the program. So there was no decision to be made.

"That really is thoughtful of you to offer all that, but I'm not interested," I responded politely.

She seemed surprised. "You're not interested in being on the *Donahue Show*"?

I restated my decision. "No, I'm not interested. I'm not interested in that type of a circus atmosphere. I've seen how you treat Christians, and I've seen how you treat conservatives. And I'm not interested."

She was quiet for a moment. "Well," she finally responded, "I'm going on vacation and I'll call you again when I get back in town. I hope you'll change your mind."

She did call back later, and I reiterated my position. "Thanks for the invitation, but I'm still not interested."

"Well, we're coming to Fort Worth anyway."

I believed she was bluffing. Besides, whether he came to Fort Worth or not, I could only assume that Donahue wanted to destroy my credibility and make me look like part of a foolish fringe group. I had been warned again and again: if you are involved in a moral campaign, be extremely selective about the programs you go on.

That night I was so excited I couldn't sleep, so I decided to get some work done. I wrote over a hundred fifty letters to sponsors—until well after three in the morning.

How energized—and how humbled—I was by the Lord's intervention. I had given up on the campaign. But He hadn't given up on me.

DONAHUE UPDATE: MAY 20, 1993

"Miss Gay USA" contest features transsexual competitors.

CHAPTER TWELVE

D-Day!

T he husband of my assistant, Sheryl Burkett, is an employee of
Southwestern Bell Telephone. On April 8, Sheryl informed me
rather matter-of-factly, "My husband is working down at the convention center today. The *Donahue Show* called his office, wanting
eighteen phone lines installed there."

Until that moment I had been in a state of denial, believing it was
highly unlikely they would actually come to Fort Worth. My denial
quickly transformed itself into a knot in my stomach. Anonymity, at
least in my own hometown, was about to become a thing of the past.

That same day Steve Smith called me and verified it. He had called
the *Donahue Show* and had learned they had scheduled several programs in Fort Worth. The one about me would be broadcast on April
14.

"They've tried to get a number of guests," Steve said, "a number of
pro-family people, but everyone has said they don't think it would be
fair. They've finally linked up two—Robert Peters, who is the president
of Morality In Media in New York City, and Monsignor James Lisante,
a Catholic priest who's also from New York."

Although I didn't say it to Steve, I told myself, "Those two are
going to get butchered."

As it turned out, I was wrong.

Steve also informed me there would be a press conference after the
broadcast. He said, "I've got an idea. Why don't you show up at Phil
Donahue's press conference?"

That was worthy of consideration. Meanwhile, I had my hands
full with the media.

A Lamb to the Slaughter?

Over the course of the campaign I had survived most interviews fairly well, with my respectability intact. However, several people had warned me about one particular reporter—a writer at the *Star-Telegram* named Bob Mahlburg. One woman flatly said, "If Mahlburg calls, just run. The guy is poison, and he's particularly hard on conservatives. He's done several cutting articles on friends of mine."

On April 9, who should call for an interview but Bob Mahlburg. "Great," I thought. "The campaign is about to take a major nosedive."

"This is a weird coincidence," I told Mahlburg, "because in the past few days several people have told me to avoid you at all costs."

He asked to come to my house, but I agreed to meet him at my office the next day. I've made it a policy not to invite reporters to my home, a policy I recommend if you have an alternative location available to you for interviews.

April 10, 1993. *Didn't want to get up today. I feel the media is going to execute me, and this is the day of the lynching.*

First the newspaper photographer arrived, and shortly after ten Bob Mahlburg showed up. As we talked, he seemed genuinely interested. "How has it been going over all?"

"Pretty well," I answered. "But I've had some tough interviews recently."

Mahlburg paused, then he said, "You haven't seen anything yet."

My heart sank.

I was guarded in my responses, as I always am with the secular media. After we talked for several hours, Mahlburg asked about my motivation for the campaign. I answered as honestly as I could. "Well, first of all, I'm a Christian, and that drives my thought patterns and my desires. My other motivation is my kids. Since we've had our kids, my perspective about life has changed."

When Mahlburg got ready to leave, I said, "Bob, I'm not asking for a story biased in my favor. I'm just asking that you be objective. Please be fair."

"I'll be fair," he promised.

All I could do then was sit and wait to see what he meant by "fair."

Program subject: "The Electronic Orgasm."

Debbie Price from the *Fort Worth Star-Telegram* also called. As a rule, Debbie is liberal, but she told me, "You're not going to believe this, but I agree with what you're doing."

"Debbie, you're right," I told her. "I don't believe it."

She explained her own concern that shows like Donahue's have gotten out of hand and that television needs to be cleaned up. The articles she wrote, which appear at the end of this chapter, were both positive and thought provoking.

Before long, fourteen articles had appeared in the Fort Worth newspapers, and Phil Donahue hadn't hit town yet.

The day tickets to the show became available, I drove downtown to the convention center, curious to see what was going on. What I saw was staggering—hundreds and hundreds of people waiting in line to get tickets for the show. They may not have known anything about me, but they certainly knew who Phil Donahue was.

On April 11, when I woke up, a sinking sensation reminded me that the Mahlburg article was to appear that day. I went out and grabbed the newspaper, well aware I could be totally slandered and made to look like a buffoon in front of all my friends, patients, and everybody else I knew.

Mahlburg's article, "Shy Dentist Unlikely Foe for Donahue," was on the front page of the local section. As I read, I kept waiting for the ax to fall. But it never did. Mahlburg depicted me as an average guy, a father, and a conscientious businessman. He was fair; in fact I thought his was one of the most fair articles anyone had yet written. I left a grateful message on his answering machine and wrote him a thank-you letter.

Meanwhile, Steve Smith was still encouraging me to attend Donahue's press conference, but I had mixed feelings about it. I found myself debating the pros and cons endlessly, and never coming to a satisfactory conclusion.

Helping Hands, New Friends

A friend of Christi's, Marianna Wilson, was aware of my dilemma and suggested that her husband could help. An advertising executive, Jim is also a lobbyist in the state legislature and knows a great deal about public relations and the media.

"You'll notice in most political campaigns," he explained, "that the person who is ahead doesn't seek to debate the person who's way behind. It's always the other way around." I'd never thought about that before. He went on, "Richard, you're way ahead of Phil Donahue. In fact, you've got him on the ropes. That's why he's coming here to debate you. If you use political wisdom, you won't talk to him. You should avoid confrontation at all costs because you have everything to lose and nothing to gain. Phil, on the other hand, has everything to gain and nothing to lose."

More specifically, Jim said, "I would strongly urge you not to do any television interviews, only telephone ones. If Phil Donahue can't get you on his show, he'll take clips from any television station you've been on. He'll play them on a big screen on his program, and he'll debate you without you even being there."

"So what do I tell them when they ask?" I had already agreed to call two television stations about interviews.

"Just say, 'I'm a very private person. I'm a father. I have a business to run. I really don't have time to be driving over to Dallas for television interviews. I would be happy to give you one over the telephone, however.'"

"What if they offer to send out a remote crew?"

"Tell them you're sorry, but you don't have the time."

Finally, Jim answered my most significant question with a simple statement: "I would strongly recommend you not show up at Donahue's press conference. You have too much to lose by being there."

That night marked the beginning of a close relationship between the Wilsons and our family. Besides having made a new friend in Jim, I was deeply touched by God's provision. I prayed quietly as I drove away from their house, "Lord, how many times have you bailed me out? You help me every time I'm confused and don't know what to do. And you've done it over and over again."

DONAHUE UPDATE: MAY 27, 1993

Program subject: Female bosses who demand sex.

Donahue: Pulling Out All Stops

The next day a full page ad appeared in the *Fort Worth Star-Telegram.*

It was evident to me, in looking at the ad, that Donahue's primary tactic was a diversionary one. Instead of addressing the real issue, "Should children be exposed to sleaze programming?" he appeared to be creating a Christian versus non-Christian conflict and shifting the focus of the show to fanaticism.

We learned later that the seating arrangements at the broadcast were carefully calculated to pit the two sides against each other. The tickets from Christian bookstores were one color, and those who held them were seated in a specific section. The other tickets were a different color, and those who had them were seated opposite the Christians. Yes, I felt it was a setup.

AN OPEN INVITATION FROM

DONAHUE

IF YOU SUPPORT THE AMERICAN FAMILY ASSOCIATION, RICHARD NEILL, D.D.S., AND OTHERS WHO BELIEVE THAT:

- TV talk shows like **DONAHUE** focus too often on SEXUALLY-ORIENTED themes

- Christians must wage a Cultural War to change TV CONTENT

- Television, movies and talk shows like **DONAHUE** contribute to the MORAL DECAY of our society

- TV producers, stations and talk shows like **DONAHUE** care about RATINGS and not the welfare of our children

WE WANT YOUR VOICE TO BE HEARD ON **DONAHUE** ! YOU ARE INVITED TO A LIVE **DONAHUE** SHOW

ON WEDNESDAY, APRIL 14, 1993

AT THE FT. WORTH/TARRANT COUNTY CONVENTION CENTER 1111 HOUSTON STREET FT. WORTH, TX

The show will air live on **WFAA-TV, Ch 8, 9-10 AM**

PLEASE JOIN US!
THE **DONAHUE** STAFF

TICKET INFORMATION

To get FREE tickets for the live **DONAHUE** show on
Wednesday, April 14 at the **Ft. Worth/Tarrant County Convention Center**
(1111 Houston Street, Ft. Worth, TX), please go to the THEATER ENTRANCE
on **Saturday, April 10** between **10 am** and **12 noon**. Two tickets per person.
Tickets will be given out on a first come, first serve basis.
Note: You must be 16 years old to attend the show. *Thank you.*

April 14, 1993. *Donahue is here, and the show begins at nine. I wonder what we'll be saying about it by tonight. I'm nervous but try-ing to trust God with everything.*

Christi and I planned to watch the *Donahue* program together. Afterwards, she would take the children and leave the house for the rest of the day. I was concerned about their safety because I didn't know what kind of reaction to expect from people around the city. We had received some obscene phone calls and mail, and I thought we should plan for the worst, unlikely as it was.

A more realistic fear centered on my reputation. I knew Donahue's goal was to discredit me. While I was nervous about that, I was also exhilarated because I knew the entire campaign was going to be over soon. For me, the broadcast was three times as exciting as any Super Bowl I'd ever watched.

As the show began, it was apparent the convention center was packed; I couldn't see an empty seat in the whole place. The crowd was raucous—cheering and jeering and making cat calls. Behind Phil Donahue, as a backdrop, was an eight-foot-high picture of my petition and an eight-foot picture of some of Don Wildmon's publications. There was also a huge picture of me—not the most flattering one I'd ever seen. Donahue was ready for battle, but his fans were more than ready; they were rabid, even hostile. My office staff attended, and when they returned that afternoon, they said they had been acutely aware of the spiritual oppression in the audience. People were cursing at them, and cursing me.

After Donahue started out by saying, "We're here in Fort Worth, Texas, because this is the home of Dr. Richard Neill," then he intro-duced the guests. Bob Peters and Monsignor Jim Lisante presented themselves impressively. Their answers were polished, and both men were alert and prepared for Donahue's tactics. They obviously knew what they were doing and successfully kept Donahue on the issue of sleaze programming and the number of children watching it.

In one strategic moment, Lisante asked Donahue, "Are you concerned about the effect this type of programming will have on children who watch the *Donahue Show?*"

Program subjects: How to strip for your lover (including a demonstration); How to have a sensual body massage; How to be a better bitch.

Donahue didn't answer.

Lisante asked the question a second time. "Are you concerned?"

Finally Donahue responded, "No, I'm not concerned."

For me, that said it all.

As I had expected, Donahue worked the crowd skillfully, stirring up conflict between the two sides. At one point, Lisante said, "With all due respect to my Christian brothers and sisters, we're getting off the issue. The issue is not whether someone is a Christian or not a Christian. The issue is 'Should children be exposed to sleaze programming?'"

I glanced at my watch. Forty-five minutes had passed. I was still waiting for something devastating to happen, but, so far, I thought the show was going well.

As the show ended, Donahue said, "By the way, only two advertisers have acknowledged pulling off my program due to Dr. Neill's efforts."

One hundred twenty-five sponsors had dropped out by then. I couldn't help but wonder—if only two sponsors had pulled out because of my efforts, why in the world had Phil Donahue felt it was necessary to bring his staff, his cameras, his equipment, and everything else to Fort Worth, Texas—all at great expense?

During the program Donahue played several clips from my interview with James Dobson and Don Wildmon. In that tape, in response to the question why I had taken on such a campaign, I had said, "Dr. Dobson, it's really my desire to stand before God and to hear Him say, 'Well done, good and faithful servant' at the end of my life. That's what

I really would like to hear." Then I went on to describe my personal spiritual revival four years before. Donahue played the whole thing.

How amazing! Phil Donahue enabled me to witness to several million people at the same time.

After monitoring Donahue's show for a year, I had become quite familiar with his style. He's always poised and on the offensive. He's cool. He's witty. However, that day he was defensive. He seemed to be at a loss for words.

At the end of the show, Christi and I looked at each other and said, "We survived." Then we took a moment to pray, thanking the Lord for another deliverance.

The Aftermath

Immediately after the program, Christi, her mom, and the kids left the house. Within five minutes the phone started ringing, and it didn't stop. I learned later on, from my brother John, that a second taping had taken place following the first broadcast. It seemed to be Donahue's desperate attempt to attack again, perhaps with greater success. It wasn't any more effective than his first try.

A familiar question played and replayed in my mind that day. "Why did God chose me for this task?" I was the least likely person in the whole city to be doing such a thing. In college, I was reluctant even to raise my hand in class. There are thousands of people far more comfortable in the limelight and more accomplished at public speaking—people who could have done a better job. Why did God pick me?

A verse of scripture came to mind: "Those who hope in the Lord will renew their strength. They will soar on wings like eagles; they will run and not grow weary, they will walk and not be faint" (Isaiah 40:31).

Throughout scripture, God repeatedly chose weak people to do His work and He strengthened them. That way, the task was clearly accomplished by His direction and empowerment, and not through human wisdom or energy.

My single-handed campaign was a modern-day example of God's timeless David-and-Goliath strategy.

Excerpts from the *Fort Worth Star-Telegram*
by Debbie Price

"DONAHUE TALKS PAST SUBJECT OF THE DAY: TV RESPONSIBILITY"

Yesterday I asked Phil Donahue whether he feels a responsibility as America's leading talk-show host to set a tone for the television industry.

Donahue said he has no apologies.

And then he looked me straight in the eye and said, "Twenty-five years ago your boss could have looked down your dress and there wasn't much you could have done about it."

Say what?

One second Donahue is waxing sentimental about future archaeologists unearthing vaults of videotape, and the next—without so much as a good breath in between—he's telling me that I would be vulnerable to sexual harassment were it not for him.

This man should run for office in Oregon.

He was talking so fast and smooth that I couldn't get a word in edgewise to ask him what my dress has to do with his shows about male strippers, sado-masochism clubs or the woman who had 2,759 sex partners. Of course, I didn't have to.

I got his point.

And so did every other reporter in the room—they've been around sleazy politicians too.

But just to be sure I wasn't being some overly sensitive feminist on a tear, I asked my colleague Steven Cole Smith what he thought of Donahue's remark.

"I can tell you he wouldn't have said it to me," Smith said.

Nor to any other male reporter in the room.

"You know," Smith said, "it's like he's got all these canned responses in his head and that one just popped out. I mean, it had absolutely nothing to do with the question."

But it had everything to do with who Phil Donahue is.

A woman asks Donahue whether the television industry has a responsibility to consider the content of its programming, and he responds by turning the question personal and vaguely sexual.

"Do you think TV should clean up its act?"

"Hey, baby, if it weren't for me and my show, you'd be fighting off lechers right and left."

Who knows? If I'd been a Catholic priest, he might have started talking about pedophilia.

Maybe Donahue looks at women and the first thing that comes to mind is sexual harassment. He wasted no time rattling off all the key names—Anita Hill, Tailhook and the boys of the Spur Posse.

The only one he didn't mention was the high priestess of sex, the star of his show "My Mother Was a Slut."

I still haven't been able to find out exactly why Donahue featured the woman who had sex with 2,759 men. Every time I bring it up, the *Donahue* people start talking about Bosnia or Nelson Mandela. It's the darnedest thing.

But I'm sure there was a good reason. With Donahue, there always is.

People don't like hearing about sex with Tootsie Pops? Hey, it happened.

People don't want to know about a woman whose husband smeared excrement all over her? It's real life. Donahue showed a clip of her from jail.

People would just as soon not get every last detail of a gang rape? How else are you going to know how horrible it was for the victim?

Is Donahue, the most influential talk-show host in

America, using serious subjects as an excuse to talk dirty during sweeps week?

Never.

Without the bright light of Donahue who knows how many incest victims would continue to suffer in silence, how many senior citizens would be all undressed with no place to go?

Donahue says his critic Dr. Richard Neill has taken things out of context. It is not fair, Donahue says, that Neill—who declined to be on the show—cuts and pastes naughty bits from shows and then sends them to sponsors.

Why, Donahue says, it isn't even Christian. He said he'd never cut up the Bible like that.

But he would use the Bible-thumpers to divert attention from the real debate about television content.

I'm not a fan of the fundamentalists, although they're fun to watch when they get going about who is a better Christian. Several of them wanted to know if Donahue is a Christian.

He told them he was raised in the Catholic Church.

"Just because you're raised in a garage doesn't make you a car," one woman shot back.

Donahue said that wasn't very Christian of her. And they were off on two hours of shouting about who was going to hell first.

That was the whole idea.

Pit the Christians against one another, turn a question about television content into a discourse on sexual harassment, dodge the tough questions.

I tried one last time to find out if Donahue has the tiniest qualms about television programming today. His shows, he says, has his name on it and he stands by everything in it.

And if people don't like it, well, democracy is messy.

"We have only one place to look for the problems that ail us," Donahue said as he stood to leave, "and that is in the mirror."

He's right about that.

"Sex keeps talk shows high in ratings, low in esteem"

There are things on television that kids don't need to see and if responsible people don't have the nerve to say, "Enough," who will?

It isn't easy to tell the television and the movie industry to clean up its act. That takes the kind of courage and daring that Donahue used to have before he went Geraldo....

"Phil has been cited again and again and again as the person who not only raises political and social issues but does them in a credible and responsible fashion," Lippert, Donahue's press relations director, said. "There are issues of sexuality that are worthy of discussion even though they may not be perceived as mainstream practices."

And that is true.

But it is also true that producers put on shows about sexpots who have 2,759 partners because they're easy and guaranteed to get the ratings.

There is a freak show on every corner.

It takes work to pronounce Herzegovinia.

I'm the last person who likes anything that smells even faintly of censorship or pressure. And I don't think moving the "Donahue" show to late night is the answer.

But it's time that the responsible people in the media, advertising, and entertainment industry take a step back and see that things have gotten out of hand.

Competition is tough with all the Oprahs and Sally Jessie Raphaels and Jenny Joneses and Jan Whitneys and Geraldos out there.

Sleaze sells. But so does fertilizer, and we don't bring it into the living room.

Children spend more time with the television than they do with their parents. I don't think it's any accident that teen pregnancies and murders are at an all time high. Kids learn what we teach.

Neill may have picked on one of the cleaner talk shows, but it is the right target.

"Donahue" sets the industry standard and when Phil has time for grannies who strip, how low will Maury go?

CHAPTER THIRTEEN

One of the Proudest Moments of the Campaign

April 16, 1993. *Paul Hetrick called from Focus on the Family. They want me to do another radio interview so I can respond to the* Donahue *broadcast.*

When Paul Hetrick reached me by phone, the first thing he said was, "We're so proud of you! Dr. Dobson and I watched the program together, and we don't think Phil Donahue told the truth. He took a lot of things out of context, particularly portions of our interview with you and Don Wildmon. It was all chopped up. Would you be interested in coming up to Colorado Springs and doing another interview?"

I couldn't help but smile. "I'd be happy to!"

"How about flying up tomorrow?"

The next day I checked into the Antlers Hotel in Colorado Springs, and the following morning I met Paul Hetrick for breakfast. It was wonderful talking to him again, reviewing the campaign's progress over the past year.

Later on, while we were in Paul's office, Dr. Dobson walked in. I stuck out my hand, but he said, "That's not good enough" and proceeded to hug me.

"Are you okay?" he asked. "How are you holding up?" He knew I had taken some hits, both emotionally and physically, over the past few weeks, and I think that's one reason he invited me back to Focus on the Family—to defend and encourage me. He was also trying to vindicate

Focus in regard to some of Donahue's accusations. He said, "We're going to have a good time on the broadcast today. I think you'll like the way it comes out."

On the air we were able to counter a number of Donahue's inaccuracies. We addressed the matter of transcript material being taken out of context. We also talked about how many sponsors really had dropped *Donahue* because of my campaign.

After the broadcast, Dr. Dobson said, "Today is the day for our chapel service. Would you like to sit in on it?"

A Heartwarming Welcome

Focus on the Family has chapel services periodically, which employees' families and friends are invited to attend. About two thousand were present that day as Dr. Dobson began to review all that had happened in my campaign over the past year, especially the *Donahue* broadcast.

I was sitting there enjoying myself when Dr. Dobson said, "I've said all this because we have a genuine, American hero in our audience today. Would you join me in welcoming Dr. Richard Neill."

He asked me to stand, and when I got up, the whole place burst into applause, whistling and cheering. Before I knew what was happening, they gave me a standing ovation. I was literally stunned. I didn't know what to do—I'll never forget that moment. I only wish Christi could have been there to share it because it was one of the proudest moments of my life.

After everyone sat down, Dr. Dobson said, "Well, that should tell you how Focus on the Family feels about you, my friend. We're pulling for you, and we're on your side. We appreciate what you're doing in standing for children and for righteousness. This isn't a fight against Phil Donahue; in fact we have nothing against him at all. It's not a battle of flesh and blood but a spiritual battle, a battle of good and evil, a culture war. Let's continue to keep that in mind."

When I drove home from the airport, a simple thing occurred. But how I wish I could have frozen it in time because it so profoundly reminded me—again—of the reason I was waging the campaign. When I turned the corner onto my street, I could see my two little girls, Lauri Ann and Natalie, waiting for me on the curb. As I stopped the car, they ran over to my door and started banging on it. As soon as I opened it, they both hopped in my lap and said, "We sure did miss you, Daddy!"

Both girls sat in my lap as we drove into the garage, with nothing more on their minds than the sheer joy of being together.

April 17, 1993. *Brenda Breslauer, a producer for* Dateline NBC, *called and invited me to be Jane Pauley's guest. I turned her down.*

When she called, *Dateline NBC* producer, Brenda Breslauer, explained that Jane Pauley had strong feelings about my campaign. Pauley had written an article recently for *TV Guide,* basically addressing the same issues, and now *Dateline NBC* wanted to do a segment about my campaign. Breslauer explained, "Jane Pauley has children, and this was her idea. We'd like you to fly up to New York for the interview with Jane. Then we'll come down to Fort Worth and do some taping around your home and office."

DONAHUE UPDATE: JUNE 7, 1993

A transsexual with breast implants and a penis says, "I get the best of both worlds. Anybody jealous?"

When I declined to be interviewed, Breslauer continued trying to convince me it would be in my best interest to appear on the broadcast. "Let me send you a copy of the article that Jane Pauley wrote for *TV Guide,"* she suggested. "Then I'll call you back, and we'll talk about it. I think that will convince you the interview will be fair."

She could read my mind. I assumed Jane Pauley and Phil Donahue were friends and that the program would be a setup.

Once I read Jane Pauley's article, however, I changed my mind. I could see by what she had written that exploitative television was offensive to her, just as it was to me. I agreed to be interviewed in early May.

Back to the Daily Grind

Letters to sponsors were still going out, and by now I had a system in place, so the process of sending them didn't take as much energy as it had eight or nine months before. However, I was completely depleted emotionally, particularly after such an intense three weeks. I had been running on adrenaline since before the *Donahue* broadcast, and I knew from experience I would eventually crash. Bloodshot eyes and insomnia were my constant companions.

April 22, 1993. *Life is so hectic now. It seems like I wake up in the morning and sprint all day long to get everything done. I do a hundred-yard dash till I go to bed at night. Then I can't sleep.*

Besides my constant investment of human energy, I had probably spent fifteen thousand dollars on the campaign by this point. I could have cut the figure down 75 percent if I hadn't been so determined to used certified mail and Federal Express during the early days. Certified Mail costs almost three dollars; Federal Express costs nine dollars. I can now see these were unnecessary extravagances.

DONAHUE UPDATE: JUNE 11, 1993

Program subject:
"Bible Thumping Parents Who Have Sex with Their Kids."

Several companies, including Nutri/System, Warner Lambert, and Lever Brothers, continued to ignore me. I had, by then, sent twenty-seven letters each to three or four executives in all three companies. And they were still stonewalling me. I was coming to the realization there was absolutely nothing more I could do.

While that was frustrating, the overall statistics are encouraging:

10 percent of advertisers will pull out after one or two letters.

10 percent won't pull out, no matter what you do.

80 percent pull out after you've sent them six to ten letters, letters which have to get progressively stronger.

The message: Don't give up!

In the Big Apple

Just days before I was to leave for my meeting with Jane Pauley, I received another call from New York City. Rand Morrison, the producer of *48 Hours*, asked me to be interviewed by Dan Rather. There was a conflict of dates, because of the *Dateline NBC* broadcast, so I had to put him off until after the Jane Pauley broadcast aired. He was so persistent and aggressive I wasn't sure I would be comfortable working with him.

April 30, 1993. *Christi and I arrived in New York.*

Although the taping wasn't scheduled until May 3, Christi and I needed a minivacation desperately, so we decided to spend a few days exploring New York and resting. Unfortunately, I wasn't exactly in the mood for a vacation, tired as I was. The closer we got to the interview, the more apprehensive I became. All my peace of mind about being interviewed by Jane Pauley had vanished.

Then, on May 2, I learned that Phil Donahue's studios are located in the same building as the studios of *Dateline NBC*. That did it—now I was deeply troubled. The proximity of the two studios made me feel as if I had walked into a trap. From that point on, I was unable to enjoy anything in New York. Poor Christi was dealing with a distracted, uptight husband who longed to be safe—and anonymous—at home in Texas.

DONAHUE UPDATE: JUNE 23, 1993

Bisexual men applaud "enjoying both worlds."

That night I wrote in my diary: "I went through major oppression all day after finding out that Phil Donahue and Jane Pauley are in the same building. I wonder if they're good friends who eat lunch together. I know that God is powerful, but I feel so weak and overwhelmed right now."

CHAPTER FOURTEEN

From Dateline to 48 Hours

To my astonishment, when I awakened the morning of the Pauley interview, I had a total sense of peace. Gone was the anxiety of the preceding days, and in its place was a sense of courage and anticipation. Only God could have changed my heart so dramatically, and He did it while I was sleeping.

I had assumed the interview would take place at NBC's studios. However, after touring the studio, we met Brenda Breslauer and Jane Pauley at the Ritz-Carlton Hotel, across the street from Central Park.

An elegant suite with Victorian-style furniture and high ceilings awaited us. The lights were extremely bright and hot, and I wondered if I would be red as a beet before we finished. Jane Pauley was pleasant enough when we met, but she toughened up considerably once the cameras began rolling.

At one point she asked, "Who gives you the right to impose your morals on other people?"

I answered that question as I had many times before. "Jane, what I'm doing is as American as apple pie. It's really just democracy in action because I'm sending the advertisers information about what's on Donahue's program, and I'm asking them if this is really what they want to sponsor. They are the decision makers in this campaign, not me. They are the ones that keep the show on the air or take it off."

She continued to hit me with rapid-fire, challenging questions, and after three hours of interrogation, I felt as if I had been grilled over an open flame. The lights were hot, and toward the end of the interview I was beginning to lose my train of thought. When we left the room, I said, "Christi, I don't think I did well."

"You did great," she reassured me, optimistic as ever.

Jane Pauley simply said, "I think some of your answers are going to make Donahue dance." Off-camera she was sweet as could be, and I realized that, by asking the most penetrating questions possible, she was simply doing her job. It was my responsibility to be ready for her. If I hadn't been, I would have been roasted alive.

After the interview, she wanted to film Christi and me walking down Madison Avenue, past the corporate offices of some of Donahue's major sponsors. As we drove there, she had some interesting things to say. It became apparent to us that most of the mainstream media, liberal though they may be in their philosophy, hold talk shows like Donahue's in genuine disdain.

I felt particularly good about one statement Jane Pauley made. She said, "You know the best decision you ever made in this whole campaign was not going on the *Donahue* program. It was a setup. Since he has the on/off switch to the microphone, it would have been a no-win situation. You were very wise."

Later on, I learned that Phil Donahue refused to interview with Jane Pauley for her segment about my campaign, but I don't know why. I sensed that once the program was edited Jane Pauley would present me in a fair light. Now I would just have to wait and see if my intuition was right.

"The Battle Belongs to the Lord!"

May 7, 1993. *A tremendous, tremendous victory in the campaign, and I had nothing to do with it. Nutri/System Weight Loss Centers has gone bankrupt.*

As a key *Donahue* sponsor on a local basis, Nutri/Systems had been strategic in keeping Donahue's advertising dollars up. They never responded to a single letter of the more than 130 letters I sent to them over a year's time. When we heard about the bankruptcy at my office, we were both awe-struck and amused. We concluded, "If something can't be accomplished by people with the Lord's help, He will eventually take it into His own hands and do it all by Himself."

About the same time we started receiving hundreds of letters, and at first we weren't sure why. As we read through them, we learned that Jerry Falwell had devoted an entire sermon on his *Old Time Gospel Hour* to the destructive aspects of media. Then he had mentioned a dentist in Fort Worth, Texas, who was trying to fight the smut. After my address was displayed on the screen, I received more than 600 supportive letters. Again I was touched and humbled by the encouragement of a network of people I would never even meet.

DONAHUE UPDATE: JUNE 25, 1993

Program subject: "Housewives Who Sell Sex over the Telephone."

The Power of Concerned Americans

Despite all the media attention I had received, some stubborn sponsors continued to ignore me. They didn't all end up like Nutri/Systems, but at least one of them experienced some intense pressure I didn't personally exert. A company called Excel Mineral Corporation manufactures pet products. Earlier that spring they had written to me, stating they were not going to drop *Donahue.* Their letter had angered me somewhat because of its unpleasant tone.

After I mentioned Excel Mineral Corporation's inflexible stance on Dr. Dobson's second broadcast, they received hundreds and possibly thousands of letters from Dr. Dobson's listeners all over the country. Then I learned that a representative from Excel Mineral Corporation had flown to New York to interview with Jane Pauley for the *Dateline NBC* broadcast. She traveled there with the intention of discussing my campaign. However, she received so many phone calls from concerned friends and relatives that she got cold feet and backed out of the interview. Before long, Excel Mineral Corporation dropped *Donahue* altogether.

That is a vivid illustration of the influence of mainstream America, and of the power of letter writing. Most people are unaware they have as much clout as they do; they are convinced they really can't make a difference. But they can.

Beyond that, some individuals believe Christians should stay out of moral debates, and out of politics, and leave television programming to the producers and the networks. Oftentimes, those same people bemoan the state of our society, saying, "The world is going to hell in a handbasket."

I respond to that by saying, "You're right. Our world is going downhill. And that's precisely the point. I believe we're going to stand accountable before God, and He's going to ask us if we tried to make a difference. I, for one, want to be able to say at least I tried!

And my efforts were continuing to pay off. By May 9, 1993, I had written over 5,000 letters, and 161 sponsors had dropped the *Phil Donahue Show.*

DONAHUE UPDATE: JULY 2, 1993

Husbands and wives compare notes on their open marriages and various sex partners.

Dateline in Texas

May 10, 1993. *Brenda Breslauer and a camera crew arrived in Fort Worth to complete the taping for* Dateline NBC. *They will visit both the office and our home to film the family. I'm not looking forward to this.*

Since Breslauer wanted to visit my dental practice that morning, I scheduled some special patients who would give the right kinds of answers. Bob Beams was one of them.

When she interviewed Bob, he raved about me. He said emphatically that he thought programs like Donahue's needed to be cleaned up, and he said all this numbed with anesthetic. He was drooling out the corner of his mouth, and his lip was drooping. This wasn't the way he wanted to look on national television, and fortunately for him, he was edited out.

After taping at my office for two hours, we headed for our home. Christi had suffered with a migraine headache all day. Despite being nauseated, vomiting, and feeling miserable, she survived the interview and actually did a wonderful job. The camera crew took footage of her walking around with the children, watching television, monitoring the *Donahue* show, and charting information. I wish they had featured Christi more, because she's prettier than I am, and I think she gave better answers.

She told me later on that she'd never had a worse migraine. I couldn't help but attribute that to another instance of spiritual warfare, and another instance where God got her through.

Breslauer and the crew accompanied the five of us to a nearby park where they filmed Christi and me playing on the slides and swings with the kids, demonstrating that we were a typical family. By that time, Christi was feeling better, and we were very relaxed.

As the crew wrapped up the day's shooting, Breslauer told me, "You're like a Norman Rockwell family." I assumed it was a compliment. At least she could see we weren't fringe fanatics but just a normal family who happens to be fed up with the sleaze and sickness that is infiltrating American homes.

DONAHUE UPDATE: JULY 20, 1993

Program subject: "Teenage Transsexuals."

"I Couldn't Ask for a Better Interview"

May 25, 1993. Dateline NBC *airs tonight. The* Fort Worth Star-Telegram *ran an article today, by Steve Smith, which mentions the broadcast. Now everyone I know will be watching. I hope my friends and patients don't tune in and see me being trashed on the air!*

The Beams and Christi's parents joined us to watch the *Dateline NBC* program. As always, I was restless, checking my watch and wondering when the ax would fall. However, as the fifteen-minute segment progressed, it became apparent they had chosen to air the least controversial questions Jane Pauley had asked me. The program portrayed me as a concerned father, and a relaxed person, not an angry fanatic.

Jane Pauley made a point of saying that Phil Donahue had refused to talk to her although he had berated me for not talking to him. She also said, "Scores of advertisers have pulled out of *Donahue,* but we've had a hard time getting any of them to talk to us."

As she closed the program, I realized I couldn't have asked for a better interview. It was almost like a promotion for my campaign. When it was over, we rejoiced and cheered. Then the six of us gathered in a circle and held hands as Christi's dad thanked the Lord for His protection and guidance and prayed for continued direction.

Another Difficult Decision

Rand Morrison, the producer of *48 Hours,* was on the phone bright and early the following day. He was, as ever, extremely aggressive. Once again, I was ambivalent about agreeing to the interview. "Call me back tomorrow," I told him. "My wife and I are going to discuss it further, and tomorrow I'll have a definite answer for you." He wasn't pleased about being put off again but agreed to call back.

That night I experienced another bout of spiritual oppression. To make matters worse, I was exhausted—physically, emotionally, and spiritually. Despite the many victories in recent weeks, my eyes continued to trouble me with chronic redness, my sleep patterns were disrupted by frequent insomnia, and I felt continually weary.

Before going to bed, Christi and I prayed, "Lord, we're very confused. We don't know if we should be involved with *48 Hours* or not. Please give us clear direction, one way or the other." Friends and advisers had given me mixed signals. Some had said, "Do it. It's a golden opportunity." Others had said, "It's a mistake. Don't do it."

I was totally confused.

God's Positive Answer

I awakened the next morning with total peace; I was going to do the interview. I made the decision and haven't doubted it since.

When I called Rand Morrison to let him know, he wanted me to fly to New York immediately to be interviewed by Dan Rather.

"I can't do that," I explained. "I've got patients all day. I've got a practice to run. This has been an expensive campaign because I've taken a lot of time away from seeing patients, and I have to work. That's how I feed my family, you know."

Morrison then agreed to come and interview me himself at an CBS facility in Dallas. Because Morrison is a producer, not a journalist, the interview was not nearly as difficult as Jane Pauley's. I was prepared for the worst, but this wasn't even close.

When I arrived home, I tallied the score for the past few days and realized eight *Donahue* sponsors had pulled out that week—a number of them after Donahue's visit to Fort Worth. Apparently many advertisers were getting cold feet about the attention the campaign was focusing on inappropriate programming.

When *48 Hours* aired on June 3, the broadcast went very well. Although it was somewhat biased in favor of Phil Donahue, at some points Dan Rather actually made me look good. We thanked the Lord—once again—for His umbrella of protection over us.

In his interview with Dan Rather, Phil Donahue was nervous and admittedly defensive. He said, "We can't broadcast the front page of the

Wall Street Journal and stay in business. It just won't sell." In other words, he was saying he had to promote sensationalism and explicit programming and adult subject matter.

If he's right, it's a sad commentary on our culture. But true or not, his words gave us a clear look at what he values. It seemed to me Donahue was saying that money and success are more important than the lives of people his broadcast touches and influences. As he had said earlier, when asked about the children who might be watching, "I'm not concerned."

Our answer to that is simply, "We ARE concerned!"

CHAPTER FIFTEEN

A Time to Fight!

June 6, 1993. *Lauri Ann, our oldest daughter, accepted Jesus Christ as her personal Savior today. In the midst of the storm, both of our girls have received Christ. I think God allowed that to happen during this time to encourage us that He was right here with us, blessing our home and family.*

Amid the continuing emotional darkness generated by the campaign, Lauri Ann's decision to follow the Lord rekindled a flame of inspiration and encouragement that nothing else on earth could have sparked. It began the month—and, in a sense, the final stage of the campaign—on a warm, joyful note.

Several days later I received a phone call from Betty Wein of Morality in Media in New York. She had good news of a different sort, concerning my campaign's trickle-down effect. A story in the *New York Post* had reported the fate of a boot company that was advertising on several of the local stations there. Their commercial was sexually explicit, and several station managers had flatly refused to air it.

In the interview with the *Post*, one of the station managers said, "There's been so much uproar over the *Donahue Show* that we feel it has had a chilling effect on this type of advertising. We're not going to carry the advertisements." Apart from the Howard Stern comment, I hadn't realized the *Donahue* campaign had made an impact in New York.

What I did realize was that WFAA had piled on new Donahue sponsors, drawn from what seemed to be a never-ending supply.

A Major Decision at WFAA

On July 15 there was only one public service announcement during the *Donahue* show. That was an all-time low, which meant that new sponsors had filled in the blanks in the advertising schedule. Six months before, I would have been devastated. By now, I had learned this was simply business as usual; the number of PSAs would soon go back up.

At this point, 192 advertisers had withdrawn their sponsorship of Donahue's show.

However, by September the campaign had really shifted into neutral; we seemed to be getting nowhere. I was praying that God would begin to move in the heart of Cathy Creany, the new station manager at WFAA. As unlikely as it seemed, my number one prayer was that the station would cancel *Donahue* altogether.

On September 13 I learned that WFAA had decided not to air a controversial new show called *NYPD Blue,* produced by Stephen Bochco, who also produces *L.A. Law.* In a recent interview Bochco had said, "I'm an equal opportunity offender. If broadcast standards didn't exist, I'd be happy."

Our friend El Arnold, with the Dallas Association for Decency, informed me that the BELO Corporation, which owns WFAA, had made the decision not to air *NYPD Blue* because, as one of their executives implied, they didn't want to deal with another campaign." Apparently, the Donahue crusade had worn them down, and they felt they couldn't handle another one like it.

Astonishing News from WFAA

A few days later I wrote my first letter to Cathy Creany, letting her know I felt WFAA had been ignoring me for a year and a half. My words were carefully chosen, but I'm sure she could sense my anger.

By that time the tide had turned again in Donahue sponsorship. On September 29, 1993, twenty-one public service announcements aired. I had been expecting a turnaround, but this was quite dramatic—it amounted to a new record for PSAs in one broadcast.

Cathy Creany called me after reviewing my letter. It turned out to be a surprisingly pleasant conversation, in part because I had complimented her in the *Fort Worth Star-Telegram* for choosing not to run *NYPD Blue.*

Once we had discussed that issue, she brought up my recent letter and astonished me by saying, "WFAA has made a decision not to renew the contract with the *Donahue Show.* The bad news is that the contract doesn't run out until December of 1994."

She also told me about the efforts the *Donahue Show* was making to change her mind. "They want to send some people down to Dallas to do a presentation for WFAA, to try to talk us out of canceling. I told them not to waste their time. We're not going to be renewing."

DONAHUE UPDATE: AUGUST 9, 1993

Program subject: "Sex with the Baby-sitter."

I could hardly believe my ears. "Is there any, any chance you'll change your mind and renew it?"

"Under no circumstances will we be renewing the program," she told me firmly. "So many *Donahue* advertisers have blackballed the program it's not worth it to try to keep it on the air."

Why Not Cancel the Contract?

This demonstrates the effectiveness of a campaign that goes after the sponsors of a television program. It cuts off the monetary supply to the local station, as well as to the show itself. Very simply, the sponsors' dollars keep the shows on the air.

Although I was very excited that WFAA would not be renewing the contract, was I prepared to continue my campaign for another fourteen months? I couldn't bear the thought of it! I prodded Creany a little further. "I would appreciate it if you would try to get out of the contract immediately." And she agreed to try.

As I reflected on our good conversation, I was reminded again how important it is that Christians be logical and rational when talking to advertisers and people in the television industry. Many of them envision us as wild-eyed fanatics, angry radicals, or poorly informed, naive people. That makes it all the more critical that we represent the Lord with dignity and self-control.

The Best News of All

As 1993 came to an end, I was counting as many as twenty-five public service announcements during the *Donahue* broadcasts, and only five, paid, thirty-second spots. By January 20, 1994, I had written 6,800 letters to advertisers and more letters to supporters than I could remember. And 221 sponsors had withdrawn from the program.

All this was encouraging, but a call from Steve Smith at the *Fort Worth Star-Telegram* really got my attention. When I answered the phone, I could sense his excitement. "Have you heard what's going to happen tomorrow? WFAA is making a statement that they will be getting out of the contract with Multimedia Entertainment and Donahue in September 1994. They're canceling Donahue early." Steve and I discussed the fact that, in all likelihood, another network would pick up the *Donahue Show* in the Dallas/Fort Worth market. But for now, the battle was won, even if the war wasn't entirely over.

On January 21, the phone rang at six in the morning. Instead of answering it at that hour, I let the recorder pick it up. As soon as I heard it was KCBI, I jumped up and flipped on the radio just in time to hear the announcer say over the air, "Dr. Neill, if you're listening right now, give us a call. We'd like to talk to you about the *Star-Telegram* article this morning, concerning the *Donahue Show*."

I rushed out, grabbed the newspaper off the front lawn, and opened it up. There, on the front page, were the headlines: "Donahue Drilled." The article explained that WFAA had agreed to cancel *Donahue* in September of '94 and that the general manager of WFAA had admitted my campaign had made the difference. It was a front page story, which had gone out on the Associated Press wire.

Within a couple of hours, I was getting phone calls from all over the country again, as when the *New York Times* article had appeared months before. My first call was to the talk show host at KCBI.

Her opening question was, "So how do you feel?"

"I feel great!" I told her. "But I really want to make this clear. God has been in total control of the campaign from beginning to end. God gets all the glory for this. I can think of eight to ten major interventions that God orchestrated throughout the time. The other thing I want to emphasize is that anybody can do this. If you can write letters, if you can organize paperwork, you can do a campaign like this.

DONAHUE UPDATE: OCTOBER 22, 1993

Program subject: "Hollywood Hookers."

"WFAA's cancellation of the *Phil Donahue Show* proves that one person really can make a difference. But for a big difference to be made in the broader area of national television programming, more people are going to have to get involved. If ten people in ten major *Donahue* markets did the same thing I've done, he'd be off the air altogether."

Once I had finished my conversation with KCBI, I started eating breakfast, and before I had finished, the Associated Press, the *New York Post*, and the *Wall Street Journal* had telephoned. From half past eight that morning until five o'clock that evening, I was on the phone non-stop with the media, as well as with friends who were congratulating and encouraging me. So many people told me they had persistently prayed for us, and in fact some had prayed for years.

Looking Back at the Battle

At the beginning I had thought if I ever got 107 sponsors off the air, as Lynda Beams had done in her *Geraldo* campaign, that Donahue would be off the air and the job would be over. Fortunately, I'd had no idea that 221 sponsors would have to pull out before the local affiliate dropped Phil Donahue.

But now the task was completed—at least at WFAA.

Looking back, I see a battle that was far more spiritual than intellectual, political, or emotional. Many times, as I came to the end of my rope in other areas, I had to rely completely on my faith. One thing is abundantly clear—the campaign would have been impossible if God had not been in it. Most of my ups and downs were the result of my weak faith; it was hard for me to believe He was controlling everything. If I had trusted the Lord totally and had been willing to believe He would take care of everything, the entire experience would have been far less stressful.

The Dangers of Trash Television

My spiritual odyssey, with all its ups and downs, proved to me again and again that I was certainly not the most qualified person to launch a campaign against exploitational television. But because I was available, the Lord used me. He needs volunteers like you and me because the battle is intense, and the enemy is formidable.

DONAHUE UPDATE: OCTOBER 26, 1993

Women describe their sexual exploits.

Most of the media warlords refuse to admit they are influencing minds, either young or old, with their immoral and anti-Christian propaganda. However, Ted Turner of Cable News Network—CNN—recently stated otherwise. Speaking to a group of international broadcasters, Turner remarked, "Delegates to the United Nations are not as important as the people in this room. We are the ones that determine what people's attitudes are. It's in our hands." [Quoted by the *American Family Association Journal,* October, 1989.]

Ted Turner, who is greatly opposed to Christianity, acknowledges how much power broadcasters have. But does he take responsibility for the results?

The media has a tremendous impact on today's society, particularly on children, as Terry Rakolta, another moral campaigner, learned. Young boys and girls, whose minds are open and impressionable, are more influenced by television than anyone else. To make matters worse, the average child watches TV more than thirty-one hours per week. Daniel R. Shaw wrote about Ms. Rakolta's efforts in the book *A Mother's Battle Against Trash TV.* He reports some tragedies that were triggered by television:

- A twelve-year-old California boy raped his five-year-old stepsister, then told investigators he was acting out a television movie. It "looked like fun" so he decided to give it a try.
- Mimicking a television commercial for a children's game, an eleven-year-old Arkansas boy shot his playmate in the neck with a 22-caliber revolver.
- A seven-year-old Oklahoma youth, acting out an incident he saw in a favorite TV cartoon, hanged himself.
- In Lancaster, California, a ten-year-old boy planted a homemade bomb at his school. He later told police he had learned how to make the bomb by watching television.[1]

Words to the Wise

You and I may be unlikely candidates as change agents. We may be unknown, untrained, and untested. But there are powerful, influential individuals forging ahead of us, concurring with our position and marking out the boundaries of the battle. A decade ago Ronald Reagan stated, "If we fail to instruct our children in justice, religion, and liberty, we will be condemning them to a world without virtue, a life in the twilight of a civilization where the great truths have been forgotten."[2]

How those words resonate in today's troubled culture! Of course we should teach our children what is right and wrong, what is virtuous and what is not, what is moral and what is immoral. But, as parents, we should also teach our children by example. Too many parents shout, "No! I don't want you watching that program!" And yet those same mothers and fathers make a habit of tuning in soap operas, or prime time sleaze, or the afternoon talk shows.

Those talk shows, such as *Donahue, Geraldo,* and others of similar ilk, are described aptly by Charles Colson in his book *The Body.*

> In this televised theater of the absurd, people are presented as insecure animals—most often likable ones to be sure—who drift through life seeking nothing more than the fulfillment of their biological urges or their insatiable need for self-esteem. And all topics carry equal weight, with no objective moral distinctions. On this stage, a transvestite husband and the teenage exotic dancer and the occasional politician or professional who somehow sneaks onto the program are all graded the same way. Their nobility or heroism is established not by what they do, but by whether they are seen as doing what they find meaningful, whether they are *doing what is right for them.* Utter that phrase on Donahue, and you are guaranteed approval.[3]

Winners and Losers in the Culture War

Unfortunately, our nation's problems are not limited to the sleaze on afternoon talk shows. If that were the case, a few dozen dedicated campaigners could clean up the airwaves. Trash television is only one of many battlefronts that must be confronted in our modern world.

Dr. James Dobson has described the moral conflict in our contemporary society as a "culture war," or a "civil war of values." He writes:

Something far more significant than money is behind the contest for the hearts and minds of children. Nothing short of a
great Civil War of Values rages today throughout North
America. Two sides with vastly differing and incompatible
worldviews are locked in a bitter conflict that permeates every
level of society.... Instead of fighting for territory or military
conquests, however, the struggle now is for the hearts and
minds of the people. It is a war over *ideas*. And someday soon,
I believe, a winner will emerge and the loser will fade from
memory. For now, the outcome is very much in doubt. [4]

Dr. Dobson believes that culture wars will not go on forever.
Eventually there will be winners and losers, and the losers will have to
submit to the winners' rules. The spoils will go to the victors, and the
spoils in this case are the minds of our future generations—our sons
and daughters and our grandchildren.

A Time to Preach, and a Time to Fight

Whenever I go to Washington D. C., I like to visit an area in the
Capitol building called Statuary Hall where every state is represented
by two statues. One of my favorite sculptures there depicts John Peter
Muhlenberg and represents the state of Pennsylvania.

Muhlenberg, a great hero during the Revolutionary War, was a
Lutheran minister in the colonies. One Sunday morning after preaching he explained to his congregation, "My friends, there's a time to
preach, and there's a time to pray, but there's also a time to fight. And
that time is now."

At that point, he stood back from the pulpit, pulled back his ministerial robes, and revealed the uniform of a colonel in the Continental
Army. He marched out on the front steps of the church and proceeded
to recruit three hundred young men to fight in the Revolutionary War.
Rising to the rank of brigadier general, he saw the war through to victory, then returned home to serve as a congressman representing his
home state.

If you see Muhlenberg's statue in Statuary Hall, you'll notice that on one side he is wearing his ministerial robes, while the other side reveals his military uniform.

Today the battle is somewhat different, but no less critical. We are in great need of John Peter Muhlenbergs in our nation. Isn't that what you and I are supposed to be? Isn't it time we left the security of the church's four walls, put on the armor of God, and headed for the front lines?

Time is so fleeting. Life is so fragile. We're only going to be here on this planet for a little while. Let's make sure our lives count for eternity.

1. Daniel R. Shaw, *A Mother's Battle Against Trash TV* (n.p.: Dogwood Press, 1992), 61-62.

2. David Hoffman, "President Calls on Schools to Teach the Basic Values," *Washington Post* (August 24, 1984): A7.

3. Charles Colson, *The Body* (Dallas: Word Publishing, 1992), 166-67.

4. Dr. James Dobson and Gary Bauer, *Children At Risk* (Dallas: Word Publishing, 1990), 19-20.

APPENDIX
Writing an Effective Letter

1. Be Original: The content of the letter should be written in your own words. Form letters, petitions, and pre-printed postcards have their place, but they do not carry as much weight as your own, personalized letter.

2. Be Legible: Typed letters are probably best in this situation because you will have to send out lots of them, but handwritten letters are quite acceptable if they are legible. If they can't be easily read, they won't get the job done. A computer is a lifesaver in a letter writing campaign.

3. Be Brief: Clearly identify the issue about which you are writing. Cover only one topic. Keep the letter to one page if at all possible.

4. Be polite: Be firm, but courteous. Anger, sarcasm, and accusations will not win any points with corporate executives. They have feelings and families, and they are open to change, but you must approach them in the right way. As the letters progress, make them stronger and increasingly firm. Try to avoid threatening boycotts.

5. Be Specific: Clearly state the action you want the executive to take. For example at the end of my letter, I always ask them to withdraw their support from the *Donahue* program in every state in which they advertise. There is no question as to what I'm asking them to do.

6. Be Informed: Get your facts straight. Give at least one reason, more if possible, for your request. Quote excerpts and include actual data to prove your point. List a number of examples so there will be no question that obscenity is involved.

7. Ask for an Answer: Ask the recipients of the letter to state their view on the subject and to let you know what action they intend to take.

8. Send a Follow-Up: If they withdraw their sponsorship of the program, send a thank-you letter. If you don't hear from them after ten days, send a follow-up letter. In each letter, always ask for a response within ten days. If you have to send five or six letters, use certified mail if possible for these later letters, to emphasize the seriousness of your concerns.

9. Be Thorough: Be sure to include your name, address, and zip code. They can't write back to you if they can't find you.

10. Focus on the Message: Don't worry about writing a "proper letter." Just word it as if you were talking to your neighbor or a close friend. It is what you say, and not how you say it, that is important. Although content is of primary importance, make your correspondence as grammatically correct as possible.

11. Choose the Right Perspective: Don't approach your subject from a religious point of view. If you do, the opposition will likely say you are trying to impose your religious values on others.

12. Know Where to Write: The simplest way to find a company's address—at least the city in which it is located—is on the label of one of their products. Call information in that city to get the phone number. Then call the corporate headquarters to find the mailing address and the names of the top three executives in the company.

Ways to Find the Information

1. Most items have the address and phone number on the product. You can start there and call the corporate headquarters. Many times they will give you the information over the telephone. Sometimes they are a little protective of their executive names, so you may have to get creative to get the information.

2. Sometimes the grocery store will have the information or can tell you how to get it.

3. Call the American Family Association at 1-800-326-4543. They have most of the major sponsors listed.

Another way to find corporate executives' names is at your local library. There are several books that list major U.S. corporations and their executives in the business reference section at the library. If you do this, make sure it's up to date.

As I mentioned in Chapter Three, The American Family Association publishes *The Fight Back Book,* which lists several hundred companies and products in an easy-to-use format.

Another organization, called Friends of the Family, based in Joplin, Missouri, has a book called *Taking on Hollywood.* This is an excellent resource guide on speaking out and fighting against television. And you can get this book by sending $5 to:

Friends of the Family
P. O. Box 2153
Joplin, MO 64803

This publication provides a wealth of information, including products and companies' names and headquarters.

13. List Sponsors Who Dropped Out. If other advertisers have withdrawn because of your campaign, list their names in the letter. This will give the targeted advertiser the feeling that large numbers of other advertisers are pulling out, and he may not want to be the only one left.

14. Keep Good Records. Be sure you retain accurate records of each letter that's sent out. Keep a letter log which details the date, the company name, and the specific letter that was sent on that date. Note the response. Organization is very important.

15. Send It in Triplicate. Address your letter to three people in each company if possible. In the larger companies, there may be more. I usually send it to the CEO, the president, the vice president of marketing, and the vice president of advertising. In small, Mom-and-Pop companies, there's usually one person, or maybe two, who should receive the letter: the owner and perhaps the person responsible for marketing.

16. Use Current Information. Always mention a handful of topics or excerpts from recent programs. This will update the advertisers about what has been on the air in the past few days.

17. Mention Your Supporters. List organizations that are backing your campaign, but be sure you have permission to use their names. State how many people are involved in the organizations—numbers are important to advertisers.

18. Inform Them of Publicity. If you are about to make a public appearance, give an interview, or hold a press conference, let them know.

Sponsor Research Information

Product Advertised:_____

Sponsoring company name: _____

Address: _____

_____

_____

Phone: _____

Name of Chief Executive Officer (CEO): _____

_____

Names and positions of the 3 executive officers next in line:

Name:_____

Position: _____

Name:_____

Position: _____

Name:_____

Position: _____

Name and position of person over public relations or advertising:

Name:_____

Position: _____

Important Points in Preparation for the Media

1. Try to get interviews with the Christian media before you have to deal with the secular media.
2. Whether you're interviewing with Christian media or secular media, the most important thing is to be prepared.
3. Determine who your audience is going to be—Christian or non-Christian, activists or non-activists, men or women. Remember, you're not really talking to the reporter or the talk show host. You are talking *through* them to the thousands of people who are listening to your message. These are the people you want to persuade.
4. Several days prior to the interview prepare a list of "good words" and "bad words"—good words that will give a favorable impression of you and your campaign, bad words will give a negative connotation to you or your cause. Some words you might want to consider:

Good Words:
   concerned parent
   strong family values
   devoted
   determined
   fed up
   protecting children
   committed
   taking a stand
   children—our most precious resource
   for a good cause
Bad Words:
   attack
   censorship
   threaten

extremist
fundamentalist
judgmental
right wing
boycott
controversial

5. Write out your key phrases, your sound bites. These are phrases you will need to use regularly.

Some of the sound bites I used:
This is as American as apple pie.
I am simply a concerned parent.
Children are our most precious resource.
I'm calling on concerned parents to stand up and be heard.
Enough is enough.
Our future generation is at stake.
I'm wanting to send a message to the television industry that we are fed up.
This is democracy in action.
I believe in rights with responsibilities.
Donahue is the tip of the iceberg.

Keep your sound bite phrases short and simple, but striking and bold. Have a number of them ready.

6. Prepare both negative and positive questions that you may be asked. Get together with friends and have mock interviews during which they ask you questions—the toughest questions they can think of. Then brainstorm the best answers possible.

7. Always stay on the issue. If a reporter starts straying away, use phrases like "The real issue is..." or "The most important point is...." Do not allow a reporter or interviewer to distract you from the subject you want to talk about.

8. If a reporter inquires about your salary, race, religion, political

views, etc., feel free to say, "That's really very personal, and I don't feel comfortable answering that." Never say, "No comment." It will sound as if you're hiding something.

9. Acknowledge the reporter's question; never ignore a question. But don't answer it if you don't want to. An acknowledgment can be as simple as a yes or a no answer. Or you can use a subtle acknowledgment phrase, then say what you want, while never actually answering the question.

Here are examples of acknowledgments:
That's an interesting question, but let me first say...
Let me put it in perspective.
I'll get back to that, but...
Before I get too deeply into a discussion of that, let me first explain...
Let me begin by saying...
I have heard that question.
I have not heard that question.
Not necessarily.

After you have acknowledged the reporter's question and given your key sound bite phrase or phrases, follow up with a statement that proves you're an authority on the subject. Give statistics from Neilsen ratings, or key facts and figures, or a story that will show how involved you are. There are many ways to show your credentials.

10. The last part of your answer is background information, which may be short or very long. Some of my background information includes anecdotes and quotes from well-known people. Other background information could include reading a letter from a supporter, or topics from various Donahue programs. Whatever background information you chose to use, you'll want it to come last. Most people who are untrained give the background information first and never get to the key sound bite which is most important.

The proper order of your answer: acknowledgment—key sound bite—statement that proves you are an authority—background.

11. Always smile.
12. Do not appear cocky or arrogant.
13. With Christian media, always try to give the listeners an action step. In my campaign, I sometimes gave the names and addresses of CEO's of one or two stubborn sponsors. I asked people to write them and encourage them to withdraw their support of Donahue. I also gave out my post office box in case listeners wanted to find out more about the campaign or get involved.
14. When interviewing with the secular media, don't be afraid to identify disgusting topics or to use quotes from some particular program. In the words of a friend of mine, "You have to make it smell bad."

    If a reporter tries to make you look like a radical or implies that you're overreacting, just say, "Wait a minute. Let me give you a few examples." Then be specific. Every time I used that tactic, the reporter ended up on my side, once he realized how bad the programming on Donahue really was.
15. Always be polite to reporters.
16. If you don't know the answer to a question, it's appropriate to say, "I don't know."

Petitioning the FCC

There are two primary ways to pressure the local television or radio station.

Number one: Persuade corporate advertisers to withdraw their advertising support.

Number two: Petition the Federal Communications Commission (FCC) to deny license renewal to the station in question.

When a large number of sponsors have pulled out, it's time to open correspondence with the FCC. Much of the following information has been taken from a report entitled "How to File a Petition to Deny the Renewal of a License to Broadcast Held by a Radio or Television Station."

This report was written by Peggy Coleman, who is an attorney with the American Family Association. Here are excerpts from the report:

> You can help change the face of public broadcasting. The process outlined below will require some work, some record keeping, and some letter writing. It can also be a most effective method of helping bring decency back into broadcasting. It is the process that involves the filing of 'A Petition To Deny Application For License Renewal.'
>
> A Petition to Deny is a legal request by an organization, or an individual, to the Federal Communications Commission, that a radio, or television station's request for license renewal be denied. Every local radio and television station is licensed by the Federal Government, to "broadcast in the public interest."
>
> Should the station lose its license, then it not only loses its ability to convey information, but it also is denied a lucrative business opportunity. The Petition to Deny is an effective step to make a station that is primarily concerned with profit responsive to the needs of the local community.

For the process to be successful, it is very important that each step be followed. The FCC will not consider a Petition to Deny that has not been properly filed. If the local station knows that you and others are working on a Petition to Deny, that you are willing to take the time and do your homework, and get the material in order, your local station will begin to examine very seriously the kind of programming it airs.

Simply by going through the steps outlined, you can effectively help curb the amount of indecent programming. Whether the station loses its license or not, the station knows that going through the process of defending a Petition to Deny is expensive and often counter-productive.

Each station seeking a renewal of the license must submit an application no later than four months prior to the date of the license expiration. Once the application for license renewal is filed, a Petition to Deny that license application renewal must be filed.

Upon filing an application for renewal, the station must give public notice of the filing. This is done through newspaper notices, and notices over the air of the licensee. The following steps provide basic guidance and suggestions for individuals who participate in the Petition to Deny project, to be heard during the re-licensing project.

Please do not hesitate to call or write the American Family Association legal staff for further information or clarification.

1. Identify the radio station and television stations in your community.

Suggestion: Use the telephone book, the entertainment section of the local newspaper, or just turn through the dial and identify the stations you can hear. Identify the stations by call letters, for example; WKYS FM or KCFC-TV. The FCC filing system is arranged only by call letters of the stations that are licensed.

2. **Identify the physical location of the station in your community.**

Suggestion: To determine the address of the station office, you will need to review the public file kept at the station for additional information. The station is required by the FCC to keep a "public file" of all letters of comment or complaint it receives from the public.

By law, the station must make this public file available to anyone who desires to see it during normal business hours. You will also need to identify the owners of the station and the station mailing address. If this information is not easily available, contact the American Family Association. They can assist you in finding it.

3. **Identify the time when the radio and television station licenses are subject to renewal.**

Broadcast licenses are issued to radio stations for a period of seven years, and television stations for five years. Again, the AFA can help in getting this information for you.

4. **You should enlist several people to monitor the station or assist in filing complaints.**

Coordinate efforts to monitor the station for violations sufficient to support a Petition to Deny. Monitoring could be a continuous process throughout the period prior to the time of renewal. The FCC accepts Petitions to Deny at any time during the four month period prior to the date of the license expiration. Monitoring, therefore, should be done most extensively during the one year period prior to the date for license renewal. Any of the licenses subject to renewal should be monitored from the present until the time of renewal occurs. The Petition to Deny will be most effective if the violations are consistently documented, and complaints are regularly filed against the station.

Suggestion: The most important role you and other members will play in this effort will be to effectively monitor and take appropriate action when indecency violations occur. Please follow these instructions to ensure accurate monitoring. When a potential indecency violation occurs, submit a tape recording, either video or audio, to the FCC along with the complaint about the specific program.

Very important note: Filing a complaint is not the same as filing a petition to deny. These are two separate processes. But before a Petition to Deny will be considered by the FCC, complaints against the station with respect to specific programming must have been filed and the FCC must have been given the opportunity to act upon those complaints. You may need to file several complaints during the course of the monitoring period.

A complaint should be filed for each time a potential indecency violation occurs. Identify any other complaints that have been filed against the station for the broadcast of indecent or obscene material since the license was last issued. You may check the station public file or contact the FCC. You'll need to refer to the station by its call letters to obtain any information regarding complaints.

5. **Assemble the information for use in filing the Petition to Deny.**

Suggestion: At a time four months prior to the renewal date, begin to assemble the information necessary to support a Petition to Deny. This will include making an additional copy of any tapes and written materials that were submitted with complaints to the FCC regarding specific incidents of indecent programming.

Identify the individual or organization who will be identified as responsible for the Petition to Deny. This individual or organization will be required to state what particular interest they have in the license renewal process. The American Family Association legal staff will assist in preparing the actual statement of interest. In addition, information about programming which was offensive, but not necessarily indecent, should be included. This may be summarized in a narrative form.

6. **Submit the information to the American Family Association legal staff for final preparation of the Petition to Deny.**

Suggestion: The Petition to Deny will be filed against the specific stations you have identified. The information you and your group obtain will be assembled with the information obtained from other sources regarding the particular station. This will help ensure that we are able to file a Petition to Deny that will be most effective. The end result should be a careful review on the part of the FCC of these applications for the license renewal.

A broadcast license is a very valuable commodity, often selling on the open market for millions of dollars. And no station will want to lose its license or even face a serious threat of losing its license. Your participation in this process should result in stations becoming more responsible in broadcasting choices.

Guidelines
for Monitoring in Preparation for Petition to Deny

The following guidelines will assist you in monitoring radio and television programs in the most efficient and productive manner.

1. Contact several friends, church members, or your Sunday school class to assist in the monitoring process.

2. Assign different hours for people to monitor. Ask them to be sure to use a VCR and/or tape recorder for documentation purposes. You may wish to use more people to monitor television since this may be more time-consuming.

3. Identify specific periods of time or particular programs that will require monitoring.

4. Identify any programs that may be indecent or obscene, and file a complaint with the FCC. With each complaint filed with the FCC, send a copy to the local station, and ask that they include your complaint to the FCC in their public file.

Filing a Complaint with the FCC

The FCC investigates allegations of indecent or obscene programming on the basis of complaints of individuals regarding specific programming. There are specific guidelines, which must be followed for the FCC to properly consider your complaint.

1. Submit a letter of complaint to the FCC, stating that you feel the material violates federal law, prohibiting the broadcast of indecent and obscene material. You do not have to identify the specific section of the law. In the letter, you will also want to call for action on the part of the FCC to sanction for such violation.

2. Identify the station by call letters.

3. Enclose a tape recording, audio for radio, and video for television, with the letter of complaint. The tape should include not only the allegedly indecent scene, but most if not all of the particular program. If you don't have a tape recording, explain the nature of the complaint as fully as possible in your letter. Include the date and the time the material was broadcast in the letter of complaint. The letter of complaint and a copy of the tape recording should be sent to:

   Federal Communications Commission
   Mass Media Bureau
   Enforcement Division
   Complaints And Investigations Branch
   1919 M Street
   Washington, D. C. 20554

4. Be sure to keep a copy of the letter and the tape recording for your files, for future reference. And be sure to send the local station a copy of your complaint letter and ask that it be put in their public file. Do not send your only copy of the tape to the FCC. Make a copy to send and keep the original in your possession.

I would suggest contacting the legal department of the AFA any time you need assistance. They were very helpful with me in my campaign, in giving me advice, and in helping with legal documents. Their phone number is (601)844-5036.

Important Pro-Family Organizations
and Christian Media Venues

FOCUS ON THE FAMILY
Dr. James Dobson, president
8605 Explorer Drive
Colorado Springs, CO 80820
Phone: 1-(800)-A-FAMILY

They publish *Citizen* magazine and air *Family News in Focus*. They
also have many other ministries.

CONCERNED WOMEN FOR AMERICA
Beverly LaHaye, president
370 L'Enfant Promenade S. W. Suite 800
Washington, D.C. 20024
Phone: (202) 488-7000

They publish *Family Voice* magazine, and air *Beverly LaHaye Live*.

EAGLE FORUM
Phyllis Schlafley, president
P. O. Box 618
Alton, IL 62002
Phone: (618) 462-5415

CHRISTIAN COALITION
P.O. Box 1990
Chesapeake, VA 23327
Phone: (804) 424-2630

They publish *Christian American* newspaper.

USA RADIO NETWORK
Phone: (800) 992-USA1

This network airs *Point of View* with Marlin Maddoux, along with news broadcasts, on over 900 stations across the country.

• More than likely, AFA, CWA, Eagle Forum, and Christian Coalition have local chapters near you. You may want to get involved with them.

FRIENDS OF THE FAMILY
Steve Head, president
Route 5 Box 365
Joplin, MO 64803
Phone: (417) 782-8842

MORALITY IN MEDIA
Robert Peters, president
475 Riverside Drive
Room 239
New York, NY 10115
Phone: (212) 870-3222

AMERICAN FAMILY ASSOCIATION
Dr. Donald Wildmon, president
P.O. Drawer 2440
Tupelo, MS 38803
Phone: (800) 326-4543

They publish the *AFA Journal* on a monthly basis. My primary contact was Allen Wildmon.

Also, you may want to contact...

• Local Christian radio stations
• Local Christian newspapers or newsletters
• Your denomination's national, state, and local publications
• Pro-life and anti-pornography organizations
• PTA and other civic organizations
• Churches

Some of the Sponsors Who Have Withdrawn
All Donahue Advertising

Abbott Laboratories
ADT Security Systems
Albertson's
American Home Products
Arby's
AT&T
A-Affordable Insurance
Baskin-Robbins
Blackmon-Mooring
Blue Cross/Blue Shield of Texas
Blue Lustre Products
Braum's
Bryan Foods
Burger King
Burlington Industries
Burns & Ricker
Buy Owner
CCA, Inc.
Carpet Exchange
Carpet Mills of America
Carter Eye Center
Cash America
Cataract Institute of Texas
Charter Hospital of Dallas
Charter Hospital of Fort Worth
Circuit City
Cloth World
Clorox Co.
Colgate-Palmolive
Combe, Inc.
Consumer Credit Counseling Service

Cosmopolitan Lady
Dalworth Carpet Cleaning
Dannon
Dean's Foods
Dial Corporation
Dillard's
Dole
Dr Pepper
Drug Emporium
Dow Chemical Co.
DuPont
Dusty Attic
Eureka Company
Everfresh Beverages
Expressions Furniture
50 Off Stores
Freeman Mazda
G. Heileman Brewing Company
Gerber Baby Foods
Glamour Shots
Hancock Fabrics
Haynes Underwear
Hillshire Farm
Hoover Co.
Hormel
HUD
Hygrade Foods
Johnson Wax
Jungle Jim's Playland
Kayser Roth
Keebler
Keyes Fibre Co.
Kmart
Kraft & Johnson

Jenny Craig
John Paul Mitchell
Lady Foot Locker
LA-Z-BOY Furniture
Lea & Perrins
Long John Silver's
Luby's Cafeterias
Macy's
MacFrugal's
Medicine Shoppe International
Minyard's
Mr. Coffee, Inc.
Mutual of Omaha
National Clinical Research Centers
National Dairy Board
National Review
Nationwide Furniture Liquidators
National Mental Health Association
Nestle USA
Night Hawk Frozen Foods
Ogle School of Hair Design
Optical Clinic
Orkin
Owen's Restaurants
Pet, Inc.
Philips Electronics
Physicians Insurance Co.
Progressive Southern Mortgage
Properties of the Southwest
Quasar
Rainbo Bread
Ralston Purina
RB Furniture
Reckitt & Coleman

Redbird Nissan
Riviana Foods
Roman Meal Bread
Room Store
Royal Crown Cola
Remington Products
Revlon
Rug Doctor
Sara Lee
Schering Plough
S & J Shoes
Seven-Up Company
Singer Sewing Company
Sports Town
Starkist
St. Petersburg/Clearwater
Tom Thumb-Page
Thorn Apple Valley
United Industries
Veterans Life Insurance
Washington Apples
Wendy's
William B. Riley Co.
Winn Dixie
Worthington Foods
Zaks